MENSA®

HOW TO

EXCEL

AT IQ TESTS

General Editor:
Robert Allen

Authors:
John Bremner
Philip Carter
Dave Chatten
Ken Russell
Carolyn Skitt

CARLTON
BOOKS

Contents

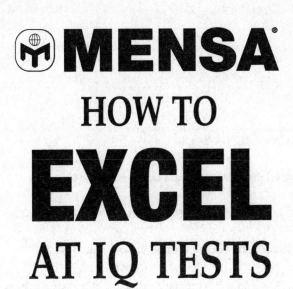

MENSA
HOW TO
EXCEL
AT IQ TESTS

THIS IS A CARLTON BOOK

Text copyright © British Mensa Limited 1998, 2002

Design and artwork copyright © Carlton Books Limited 2002

This edition published by Carlton Books Limited 2002

A CIP catalogue for the book is available from the British Library

ISBN 1 84222 685 1

Project Editor: Martin Corteel
Project Art Direction: Darren Jordan
Production: Sarah Corteel

Printed and bound in Great Britain

Based on material taken from *Mensa - Challenge Your IQ* (1998) and
Mensa - Mind Assault Course (1998).

Introduction

Although IQ testing has been with us for many years and still remains controversial, it is regularly used as a way of selecting people for employment and promotion. Whatever reservations psychologists have about what intelligence is and how it should be measured, having a high IQ is still a sure way to gain the attention and respect of people who exercise influence over your life. This book has one simple aim, to show you how to maximise your IQ score. For while it is not possible to increase the brainpower with which you were born, it is relatively easy to show you ways to extract every last bit of advantage from the intelligence that you have.

An IQ test is just another sort of exam and, like all exams, there are rules that can be exploited to the candidates advantage and techniques that will help to achieve a better score. None of this is cheating, it's just good exam technique. What follows will help you sharpen your wits, increase your thinking speed and get used to the sort of mental obstacle course that leads to an impressive IQ score.

If you are interested in IQ you will like Mensa, a society that exists entirely for people with an IQ in the top 2% of the population. The society has well over 100,000 members throughout the world and offers a huge range of social activities. If you would like to take the Mensa test and meet people of like mind, thenwrite to British Mensa Limited, St John's House, St John's Square, Wolverhampton WV2 4AH, England, or American Mensa Ltd, 1229 Cor[orate Drive West, Arlington, TX 76006-6103, or contact Mensa International, 15 The Ivories, 628 Northampton Street, London N1 2NY, who will be happy to put you in touch with your own national Mensa

About intelligence

Intelligence has many definitions. In 1923 it was wryly defined by the psychologist Edwin Boring as "That quality which intelligence tests measure." And things are exactly as simple and as complex as that. IQ — our intelligence quotient — is a difficult thing to pin down. IQ tests are scorned by some as testing only the ability to do IQ tests, but many of the abilities involved in the completion of IQ tests have proven to be very useful in our daily lives. The various abilities of logical thinking, problem solving, dealing with the language that we use every day, and manipulating numbers and shapes are the same abilities which, when combined with emotional reasoning, make us effective human beings.

Another psychologist, Ulric Neisser, recently defined intelligence around the concept of an *ideal prototype*, with people being more or less intelligent according to how closely they approach the prototype. There are two ways of achieving a prototype. The psychometric prototype is statistical where we simply say that a perfect score is 1 and this becomes the ideal prototype. We are scored according to our deviation from that score. This is close to the method used to score most IQ tests currently in use where the IQ score is the deviation of a person's score on a test from the mean test score of a reference population, divided by the standard deviation. In other words, the rating which you achieve on an IQ test is compared with the rating which everyone else achieves, and your score is weighted according to the results of others. By definition according to the convention of scoring, the average IQ is 100, and we know that fifty percent of the population will score between 90 and 110. But if, on a particular test, it were found that the average of all tested was 90, the weighting would be adjusted to bring the average back up to 100. Thus are tests standardized. Looking at the sample figures below it can be seen that if all points were plotted, the classic bell-shaped curve would be evident. More on that later.

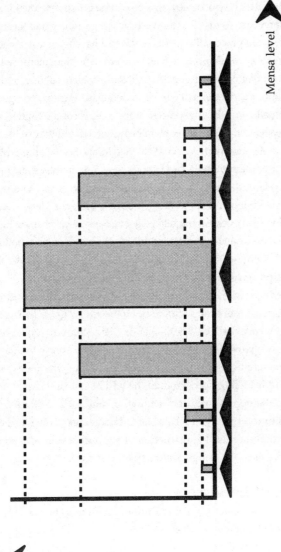

50% of the population have IQs between 90 and 110. Only 2% have IQs lower than 53 or higher than 147.

Mensa level

Percentage of Population

The other way of achieving a prototype is to define the ideal intelligence in terms of cognitive-psychology, where intelligence is viewed as a process. To do this we would have to choose the ideal processes of intelligence such as problem definition, memory storage, mental imaging, resource collection, and problem solving, and we would also have the dilemma of having to define the ideal prototype use for that intelligence. But the processes are complex and infinitely varied according to the type of problem being solved and we can be specific only to the environment in which we operate. Solving the problem of, say, stopping somebody from shouting at you, involves few of the processes of defining the difference between, say, paper and metal foil. As to environments, a physics genius may have the ideal intelligence for making discoveries about relativity or quantum mechanics, but be unable to survive in a desert where the average nomad who has never heard of physics, thrives happily. But take the nomad out of the desert into a physics laboratory and the situation is reversed.

Perhaps with something like the above example in mind, intelligence has been defined by H. Woodrow as "The capacity to acquire capacity;" by S.S. Colvin as "The ability to adjust oneself to the environment;" and by R. Pintner as "The ability to adapt oneself adequately to relatively new situations in life." In other words, if the nomad is an intelligent nomad, he will be able to learn about physics, given the opportunity and inclination, and if the physics professor finds himself in the desert, if he is an intelligent physics professor and comes under the instruction of a group of nomads, he will be able to learn the things necessary for survival.

Types of Intelligence

What Woodrow, Colvin and Pintner all seem to be identifying has come to be known as *fluid intelligence* — the combination of qualities measured by the Cattell test used by Mensa, and the same qualities which have ensured our survival as a species and the lack of which causes the downfall of species less able to adapt to changing circumstances. This combined intelligence aspect has great relevance in everyday life, particularly in today's changing job market. Versatility is the most important asset of potential employees. What you are capable of now matters more than what you have done in the past. There have been a number of cases where very high fliers have been enticed away, for huge sums of money, from jobs where they were achieving spectacular success, in the hope that they could bring that success with them and turn failing businesses into successes, only for them to become equally spectacular failures in their new positions. Where did things go wrong? Why cannot future success be measured by past performance?

The answer is that it may have taken years for them to learn how to be good at their last job, and during those years they will have accumulated judgement, wisdom, and thinking skills specific to that job and situation. But in the case of those somewhat lacking in fluid intelligence, only specific to that situation. Their new employers have failed to realize that someone who has spent the last twenty years learning about, say, steel may have achieved that success by hard work and determination and by learning the hard way — from mistakes. A better way to choose a new company leader who would not spend the first five years learning from mistakes would be to test the fluid intelligence of every reliable and hard-working employee already working for the company and promote the person with the highest score into the position! Well, perhaps not, but the lesson should be learned that people can have achieved success despite being dull thinkers and perhaps in some cases because of it. Traditional methods usually work for someone who knows what to do, but ask the same person to do original thinking or to apply old methods to a new situation, and chaos can result.

Thus, in the workplace, the ability to learn a new job is more important than what the applicant already knows. Most employers who understand this, and who require thinking skills and judgement as employment prerequisites, have moved from measuring general and acquired knowledge — which is really a measure of memory and past experience, to IQ tests, which are a better measure of future learning ability and judgement.

Unfortunately though, fluid intelligence is not perfectly measured by psychometric IQ tests. Flexible and effective managers may not always have high IQ ratings, but they know how to deal with people, sort out problems, make fast decisions, and perhaps keep a factory in all its complexity in operation. Aptitude and personality tests may also be necessary. As another example, to obtain their taxi licence, taxi drivers in London need to have acquired 'the knowledge' — a mental map of London which enables them to go by the shortest or fastest route from *a* to *b* anywhere in the city.

Few of these taxi drivers are likely to have astonishingly high psychometric IQs, and their intelligence may not be truly fluid, but they have very high knowledge-based intelligence specific to their job, which takes a great deal of hard work and determination to acquire and which gives them an advantage over other drivers in London who may have much higher psychometric intelligence. There will be also be some crossover of their skills and acquired intelligence into everyday life. Visual-spatial intelligence — which taxi drivers must necessarily acquire, is thought by many experts to be the aspect of intelligence which gives the most accurate score of natural non-culture-based intelligence. In the case of taxi drivers, this may not always hold true, but it is likely that their increased visual-spatial skills will have the effect of increasing their overall IQ score.

But like the brilliant manager or company director with knowledge-based crystallized intelligence who is recruited by another company, if the taxi driver were transported to a strange city he would be less effective for a considerable time than the locals. The taxi driver's job-specific intelligence does not have the same survival value as the previously mentioned nomad's fluid intelligence. That said, knowledge-based intelligence is highly valued by our society and is of more value to an individual who uses it than high psychometric IQ to an individual who does not use that potential. In the end, what we do with our intelligence matters more than the type or quantity of intelligence we have at our disposal.

Divergent and convergent thinking

If you have good fluid intelligence, you will be good at divergent thinking — the process of finding previously undiscovered solutions to problems, whatever the type of problem you tackle. It can take the same kind of creative intelligence to find a workable solution to a family crisis as to find a cure for a disease, or to invent a new type of engine. The tools you need to solve problems with divergent thinking are originality, adaptability, fluency, and inventiveness, and the typical divergent thinker will usually explore many possible solutions before finding the best one. It may even be true to say that only a divergent thinker can do this.

A convergent thinker is likely to pick the first viable solution that is found, and stick to that no matter what happens. Divergent thinkers have multi-track minds. Convergent thinkers have one-track minds. Henry Ford's famous slogan about the model T Ford, "You can have any color so long as it is black," is typical of a convergent thinker, but Ford was a good convergent thinker, so he surrounded himself with divergent thinkers and he had a row of buzzers on his desk to summon the thinkers he needed to solve his problems. Again typical of convergent thinkers, Ford was very stubborn. Despite being told that an eight cylinder V8 engine block was technically impossible, he instructed his engineers to design and make the engine and he repeatedly refused to take no for an answer. He had picked his first viable solution and nothing was going to change his mind. It took over a year for his design team — divergent thinkers

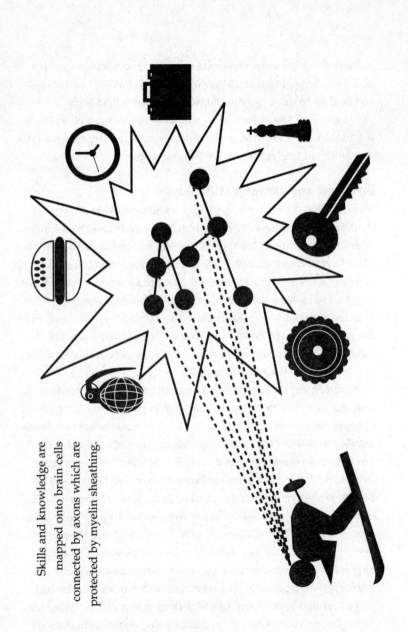

Skills and knowledge are mapped onto brain cells connected by axons which are protected by myelin sheathing.

to a man — to come up with a solution, but when they did it took the motoring world by storm. The force of combined divergent and convergent thinking working together is hard to beat.

Physical Changes

Contrary to popular belief, the brain undergoes physical changes in the process of learning. We can't make more brain cells, but we constantly make new connections between those cells in a network many thousand times more complex than the world wide telephone network. Knowledge increases that network of connections as does acquired skill and improved mental capacity of every kind. Recent studies have shown that even fluid intelligence can be improved by exercising the brain. Each cell in our brain can have up to 10,000 connections, some of which get priority over others. When we use a connection route a lot — when we learn things permanently — our brain decides to protect that connection and coats the connections with myelin, enabling faster and more reliable chemical and electrical communication. Thus, old people with Alzheimer's disease, who have forgotten everything they have learned over the past sixty years, may still be able to recall verses learned by rote in childhood, the memories protected from the ravages of Alzheimer's by myelin sheathing. Thus also, recurrent nightmares and bad memories. When something terrible happens to us, our brain ensures that we don't forget it by coating the relevant connections in myelin. This is a defense mechanism to try to prevent recurrence of the harmful circumstance. But these are mapped into cerebellum; not really like cerebral memories above (in these examples, the cerebellum at the base of the brain).

This also explains why exciting lessons are easier to learn that boring ones. The brain does not invest much construction time creating new connections or protecting connections for things that apparently do not matter. Everything that happens in the brain is a matter of survival priorities. Only if something matters to us so much that we keep returning to it does the brain build protected connections to that information or skill. This is why very slow readers, like those with dyslexia, who keep having to go back over the material, when they do get through a book, know it much better than a fast reader who looked at each word only once. Because of their very short term memory for words, some dyslexic people have to learn each sentence as we would learn a poem by heart, a few words at a time. Only when they have memorized the whole sentence in this way do they make sense of it, but to do this their brain must invest in some myelin engineering. Dyslexic actors, once they have learned their lines, are most unlikely to forget them.

Learning by rote, sneered at by many, has its uses, and not just for people who are dyslexic. We can all make use of myelin engineering.

Music

A study by neurological scientists at the Universities of Wisconsin and California, of 78 three and four-year-olds from various social and economic backgrounds, showed them performing 34 per cent better than other children in IQ tests after being given simple piano lessons for six months. This is myelin engineering in action. The children appear to have gained their IQ advantage by the exercise of translating notes on paper into music on the keyboard. This is a vital time for the creation of neural networks — the pathways of our thinking. The repetitive nature of learning music seems to give just the right kick-start to the growth and myelization of the vital axons that communicate with other parts of our brain responsible for spatial-temporal reasoning. Quite why music should have this effect, nobody yet knows, but it makes sense to take advantage of such a massive IQ boosting effect — on its own enough to more than compensate for many other disadvantages.

Genetic Components and the Bell Curve

Around 60% of our IQ potential is inherited from our parents. The remainder is affected by social and environmental factors such as living conditions, parental encouragement and mental stimulation, access to learning materials, such as in the music effect above, and nutrition. It is less likely, for example, for poor people to have access to a piano. People who lead less privileged lifestyles, wherever they live, tend to have lower average IQ levels. Animal studies have also shown that the growth of dendrites and axons in the brain — the wiring of the brain network — is dependent upon these environmental factors. Without the wiring in place our brain cells cannot communicate with each other — we cannot think. However, since our IQ can be damaged by the environment in which our brain has to operate, it follows that it can be enhanced by improving those conditions and in fact we can see this taking place. As social conditions improve throughout the developed world we see a rise in IQ levels. We may be smarter as a race and as we get smarter, it may be more likely that we pass smarter genes down to our children and the cycle continues. Good so far, but a snag arises with this cycle. A healthy lifestyle in today's world is mostly achieved through wealth. We are forced to the conclusion that the wealthy will be getting smarter while the poor will not.   Recent controversy has entered this arena with the publication in 1994 of *The Bell Curve* by Herrnstein and Murray.

Based upon long term accumulation of psychometric IQ test information and upon a survey of more than 12,000 people from all social groups in the USA between the ages of 14 and 22, Herrnstein and Murray have come to the conclusion that the intelligence bipolarization is actually happening and will continue to accelerate unless we take drastic action to stop it. The book raised a storm because people do not like this conclusion. Politicians do not like it because they are, to a large extent, responsible for the living conditions of our society. The poor do not like it because it shows them to be less intelligent. Ethnic minorities do not like it because in some societies they are among the poorest and controversial claims have been made that the cause of the IQ differential is ethnic rather than wealth based. The wealthy do not like it because they would have to pay more tax to improve the living conditions of poor people.

In the end what matters is not whether people like the conclusion, but whether it is true and if so, what can be done to solve the problem. Unfortunately there is no easy solution. The poverty trap is also to some extent an IQ trap. British Mensa's recent census of members showed that the unemployment figure for Mensans is less than half the national average. Since Mensa is discrimination-free — passing a tough supervised test is the only way in — Mensans are a fairly representative sample of the top 2% of the population. This means that the less intelligent you are, the more likely you are to be unemployed — in other words, low IQ leads to poverty. Here then is the so-called Catch-22 — poverty leads to low IQ. Thus the concerns raised by *The Bell Curve*. For those in the poverty trap there seems no way out. To get out they need higher IQs. To have higher IQs they need, according to Herrnstein and Murray, to be wealthier.

This isn't strictly true because we know that about 8% of those in Mensa have incomes that are either close to the poverty line or below it, so just as it is possible to be wealthy and intellectually challenged, it is possible to be intelligent and poor. Thus, looking at the population as a whole, if Mensa is representative of the distribution of intelligence and poverty in society, we can extrapolate that perhaps 0.16% of the population will have Mensa level intelligence and be living in poverty.

Compare that to the 13.9% in the USA, who in 1996, according to the Economic Policy Unit, were earning at or below poverty level wages. In the UK the poverty figure is variously estimated at

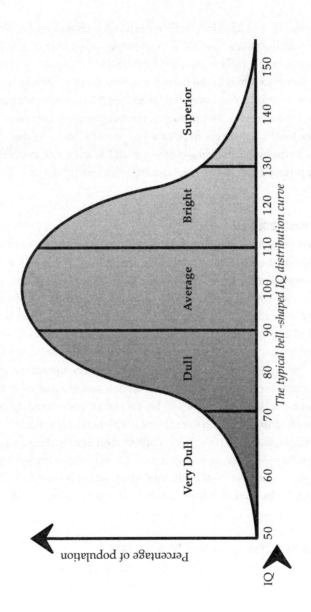

The typical bell-shaped IQ distribution curve

between 18% and 25%, but the European criteria is different, with the poverty line estimated as half of the average wage rather than at a minimum hourly income level as in the USA.

However we arrive at the figures it is clear that you are much less likely to be poor if you have an IQ in the top 2% of the population, and it would be a fair assumption to say that the more intelligent you are, the less likely you are to be living in poverty. Thus, we are forced to the conclusion, like Herrnstein and Murray, that to get rid of the *poverty equals low IQ equals poverty* cycle, we need to improve society.

Unmeasurable IQ

It is not possible to measure musical aptitude or artistic talent in a standard IQ test. Neither is it possible, through an IQ test, to measure the many and various craft talents and skills — some of which require very sophisticated thinking. A carpenter, beauty consultant, printer or hairdresser needs to be able to look at any job, estimate its cost and how long it will take, work out the materials required, figure out how to do the job, and then negotiate with the person who wants the work done. The job has to be skilfully completed, working with a variety of different tools and materials and in many cases the person undertaking the work will have a greater understanding of the practicalities of the job than others with less skill but much higher measurable IQ ratings. In Scotland there is an architect who designed a roof in such a way that it could only be constructed if it were put in place before the building which was supposed to support it. The builder redesigned the roof with the comment that the architect was "All brains and no common sense."

Individual Strengths and Weaknesses

Working through this book you may discover that you have greater numerical than verbal skills, or that your ability to work with shapes

— *visual-spatial intelligence* — is your greatest strength. We each have individual strengths and weaknesses. The important thing is to recognize our own abilities and apply ourselves to the things that we do best. Many talented writers claim to be hopeless with numbers, and there are mathematicians who cannot spell and surgeons who have brilliant memories and wonderful visual-spatial ability but who cannot operate a video recorder. This book will help you to recognize your strengths and weaknesses.

Learning Styles

In addition to the division of problems into types as shown here, there is another factor to bear in mind. Educational psychologists have become increasingly interested in the different ways that individuals learn. The most basic division is into Listeners, Lookers, and Doers. School children are now tested regularly to discover which of these is their dominant learning mode, so that they may play to their strengths. Obviously the way in which you learn will have an effect on the way in which you tackle puzzles. Listeners will tend to feel more comfortable with words, Lookers with visual problem, and Doers with anything that has some practical application. You are probably aware which is your favourite learning mode but, even so, it would be worth taking a test (there are many free ones available on the internet). The reason for this is twofold: it is important to know which is your least favourite mode. For example, if you almost never use your visual learning style is that because you have an eye problem you are unaware of? If not, and you have just never bothered to develop that particular faculty, perhaps you could add to your armoury of mental weapons by practising visual skills.

Look at the following problems and see which you can do most easily:

(Answers on page 370.)

Puzzle 1: Visual-Cognitive

All blocks not on the bottom row are supported by blocks underneath.

How many blocks?

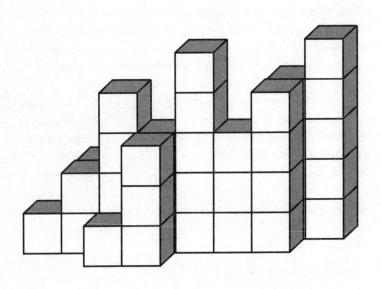

Puzzle 2: Numerical

Continue the sequence:

$$2, \quad 3, \quad 5, \quad 10, \quad \underline{}$$

Puzzle 3: Logical

True or false:

Some buttons are seagulls. Some chariots are seagulls. Some buttons are bananas. Some chariots are bananas. Therefore some bananas are seagulls.

Puzzle 4: Verbal-Linguistic

Pick the odd-word-out:

multitudinous, variegated, dappled, polychromatic, versicolored.

There are various other aspects or 'domains' to IQ, some measurable, some not. Earl Hunt, in his essay "The Role of Intelligence in Modern Society" sees intelligence as a conceptual variable and points out that the way intelligence is measured — the operational definition of that intelligence, will affect the results achieved.

Other variables involved in measuring intellect mean that it is impossible to pin an individual down to an IQ score with any degree of certainty. From day to day in comparable tests, the same person may have a measured variance of as much as thirty IQ points. Among the things that may affect your score are emotional well being (the happier you are the higher your score is likely to be within your own personal limits); circadian rhythms (sleep patterns); blood sugar levels (dependent upon the food you eat); physical fitness (studies in Manchester University have shown that the same person can score twenty points more in a comparable IQ test just by getting fit); test sophistication (the more you practice IQ tests, the better you are likely to score); and personal expectations (positive thinkers who expect to do well are likely to do better than negative thinkers who expect to fail). There are many other factors involved. Our ability to think clearly is easily affected by illness or its after-effects. It would also be foolish to take an IQ test when tired, or with Valium or marijuana or alcohol in your blood. Thus, to achieve the optimum score, it helps to do some thinking ahead.

Motivation

A high IQ is an asset in this world, but it is only one aspect of personality, and it is often the least important aspect. Studies within Mensa and elsewhere have shown that people of high intelligence tend to be more conventionally successful than people of lower intelligence, and it has been shown that IQ and earning capacity are directly related, but not everyone who has a high IQ chooses to go down that route. You may choose not to plan your time, preferring a leisurely or disorganized existence. Success means different things to different people and to those of high intelligence and sensitivity, the quiet life can be seen as having greater value than material success. Desire for personal achievement in conventional terms has to be measured against the value of peace of mind, more unplanned free time, better family life, and perhaps, escape from the rat race. High IQ thus brings the freedom to choose in the same way that money brings freedom.

On the other hand, many people with relatively low IQ scores achieve a great deal in this world. Most people have some idea of their own limitations and will compensate for those limitations by working harder. In school and college, given an intellectually gifted student who is not motivated to work and a student with an average IQ who has a high degree of motivation, the average student will usually achieve the best results. Albert Einstein, despite having an IQ of around 169, initially failed the entrance exam for Zurich Polytechnic. Fortunately for Einstein, and for the world, he had the motivation to work at the things he enjoyed and 14 years later he became a professor at the same university.

Stories of success after failure are common among the highly intelligent. W.C. Fields, the sharp-witted comedian, lost his lifetime's savings after the age of 60. Instead of giving in to despair, he used his fluid intelligence and applied his talents to a new area — the emerging moving picture industry. He soon regained his fortune. Thomas Edison tried many thousands of combinations before he managed to get a working light bulb that was reliable. John Creasey had over 600 rejections before he got his first book published . . . If you are smart enough you will eventually learn what to do to achieve the success you desire.

We often find that when a person applies effort in the area which they enjoy most, they excel. But when they apply their efforts unwisely, they fail. Epicurus (300BC), put this best when he said,

> *"Every man should examine his own genius,*
> *and consider what is proper to apply himself to;*
> *for nothing can be more distant from tranquility*
> *and happiness than to be engaged in a course of*
> *life for which nature has rendered us unfit.*
> *An active life is not to be undertaken by an*
> *inactive person, nor an inactive life by an active*
> *person; to one, rest is quiet and action labor; to*
> *another, rest is labor and action quiet.*
> *A gentle man should avoid a military life, a bold*
> *and impatient man the easy; for one cannot*
> *brook war, nor the other peace."*

Making sure all the square pegs are in square holes and the round pegs in round ones has become a major preoccupation for the human resources industry. It makes good business sense to have people in jobs that they enjoy. In addition to IQ testing, there are now many different type of psychometric tests that assess personality and job suitability. Although these can be expensive to do privately, they are frequently well worth the money, especially if your career is going through a sticky patch. Knowing for sure where your abilities lie, and which areas you should definitely avoid, is worth hard cash. Many people slog away at a career for which they, or their parents, thought they were suited and fail to notice that they would be much happier doing something else.

Test your personal motivation by completing the following quiz:

	A	B	C
Not true: 0 points → *Sometimes: 2 points* → *I believe this: 4 points*			
I am a self-made person.			
I am a good time-keeper.			
My work is very important to me.			
I plan my way ahead and follow the plan.			
I read motivational literature.			
I believe in positive thinking.			
I compete to beat others.			
I feel superior to other people.			
I make decisions quickly and stick to them.			
I keep a tidy workspace.			
Other people look up to me.			
I never get despondent.			
I keep myself fit.			
I am ambitious.			
I make my own luck.			
I complete tasks that I begin.			
I rarely procrastinate.			
I know what I want and I get it.			
I use my good ideas.			
I feel very self-assured.			
Column Totals			
Score = A+B+C			

Scoring: 80 - 60 points
Excellent. You have very high motivation and will undoubtedly succeed.
40 - 58 points
Very good. You are likely to do well in life.
20 - 38 points
You have some motivation, but need to think more positively.
00 - 20 points
You are not interested in success. Relax and have a great life.

The Drawbacks of High Intelligence

High intelligence can actually be a handicap. Clever students may be bored by the lessons and spend their time daydreaming or being disruptive. Einstein's teacher of Greek once told him, "You will never amount to anything." Einstein was a teacher's worst nightmare — he asked questions which they could not answer. Although he has claimed to be a "poor student", in fact he was top of the class in subjects which interested him. What really bored Einstein were dull uninspiring lessons, and he says, "I preferred . . . to endure all sorts of punishments rather than learn to gabble by rote."

He became so disruptive that at the age of fifteen, he was asked to leave Luitpold Gymnasium, being told that his mere presence spoiled the respect of the rest of the class for the teacher.

Faced with a child of high intelligence, parents and teachers can feel inadequate and may try to redress the balance by unconsciously bringing the child back down to a subordinate position. The cure for this problem is to be aware of it. Too many gifted children still go through school with their abilities unrecognized and may give little or no indication of their giftedness. They may even give a negative indication and have learning difficulties caused, among other things, by an inability to apply themselves to work which they find boring. It can take a lot of effort to constantly stimulate the mind of a gifted child.

High IQ children often suffer from their peers too. Nobody likes to be made to feel inferior, and children can be particularly cruel in their attempts to redress the balance. Physical and mental bullying can destroy the sensitive ego of an intellectually gifted child. With this in mind the Mensa Foundation for Gifted Children (MFGC) and other such organizations do valuable work in teacher training and in assessment, counselling and support of gifted children.

A high IQ can also be a drawback in the workplace. Employers may fear to take on anybody more intelligent than themselves in the same way that Napoleon was reluctant to allow nobody taller than himself in his presence. A survey of a hundred companies recently showed that it is best not to mention membership of a high IQ society on a job application.

Intelligent people also tend to find it more difficult to fit into a comfortable place in a less intelligent society. With an IQ of 145, you are in the top three percent of the population, which means that you may have no friends or acquaintances that can talk to you on your own level. That is not quite enough to get you into Mensa, but you are likely to be the only one in your class or on the factory floor or in the office with an IQ of that level — including the teacher or the boss. That is bound to lead to a feeling of isolation. Thus, many high IQ people have learned to hide their intelligence. Students may deliberately give wrong answers in order to fit in with a class of lower intelligence. Adults may pretend to be amused by the crude jokes and prejudices of their workmates. Anything to conform.

In the words of Cecilia Francesca de Arrom, who wrote as Caballero, "Intelligence is a luxury, sometimes useless, sometimes fatal. It is a torch or firebrand according to the use one makes of it."

Fortunately the compensations of having a high IQ usually make up for the drawbacks. Intelligent people get more out of life. They have more insight into the world around us and are less likely to make the sort of mistakes which ruin lives. Hence, if they come to terms with their intelligence and find some form of intellectual release, they tend to live happier and more productive lives than their less intelligent counterparts. A 45-year study of 1000 high IQ children in California by Professor Lewis Madison Terman showed that compared to a control group they did better in every way. They earned more, had better standards of living, were less likely to turn to crime, and even had more stable relationships.

Social intelligence

Intelligence is not, of course, necessary for happiness. Even with a low psychometric IQ, If you are good at getting on with people, you are likely to be more content than someone who has a higher IQ but is no good at relationships. This is social intelligence, or SI, and it can be a very useful asset. Life is a relationship continuum and thinking skills go far beyond the ability to do puzzles. High SI individuals can often do better in life than those who have high IQ without much SI. That said, rather too much has been made of the differences and not enough of the convergences. It has to be said that it would be unusual for very high SI to exist in a person with a low IQ, and the reverse is also true. It happens, but it is not the norm. Thus, the categorizing of high IQ individuals as cold and calculating and high SI individuals as warm and caring is a false dichotomy.

It is much more difficult to measure SI than IQ. SI tests are usually of the self-analysis type such as the previous Personal Motivation Test. The results depend on the individual being truthful. Few people will willingly admit that they are cold and calculating. We are all capable of self-deceit. How many of us would fail an exam if we were responsible for marking the exam? It is not difficult to know which answer of the choices given in an SI test would be the preferred one, just as in a Rorschach ink-blot test it would be preferable for purposes of establishing your sanity to see a butterfly sitting on a wild rose rather than a vampire bat sucking your mother's blood.

Creative Intelligence

If you are more intelligent than average, there is a 50% chance that you will also be more creative than average. However, many creative people do not have high IQs and they still manage to achieve works of great merit. It is more difficult to measure creativity than to measure IQ. A standard test for creative intelligence would be to ask you, for example, to name twenty new uses for a pail of water. Do that now. You have 5 minutes (write your results on the table overleaf):

Scoring The Bucket Test

Your thinking may be unique and highly creative, or mundane and easily thought of, and your creativity is likely to be proportional to the unique, useful and creative nature of your answers. In particular the usefulness of your answers can indicate whether your unique thought processes are the result of rational or irrational thought. Sociopaths may have unique uses for a bucket of water, but those uses are likely to involve drowning animals, committing suicide or murder, gaining revenge on those whom they feel have done them an injustice, and torture. If your answers are like that, get help!

Those who are creative but more rational are more likely to think up funny uses, or uses that could be of benefit to society as a whole, such as to pour over someone who is suffering from sunstroke, to cool the feet of those who failed at a firewalking ceremony, to use as the pendulum on a large clock, to throw over a streaker who was disrupting a game of football.

Since The Bucket Test is an open question to which you could make any reply, it would be impossible to score your answers in any definitive way here. Get someone whose judgement you trust to score the test using the following guidelines:

Score one point for every good original and useful answer.
Half points, or no points for less good answers, depending on originality and usefulness.
No points for sociopathic answers.

15-20 Points:
You are a highly creative individual. Your creativity could make you wealthy.
10-14 Points:
Very good. Your creative skills will prove useful to you.
05-09 Points:
You have some good ideas. Don't let them go to waste.
00-04 Points:
Creativity is not your strong point, but you probably have many other talents.

The Bucket Test

1
....

2
....

3
....

4
....

5
....

6
....

7
....

8
....

9
....

10
....

11
....

12
....

13
....

14
....

15
....

16
....

17
....

18
....

19
....

20
....

Creativity and Functional Disorders

There is some link between creativity, intelligence, mood disorders, and functional impairment. Dyslexia is unusually common among the creatively intelligent. It is as though the brain has compensated for having problems with reading and word recognition by overdeveloping some other areas, just as a blind person may develop extraordinarily acute hearing. Manic depressives too, may produce highly original and even brilliant work during their manic phase and discard it as useless during their depressive phase, only to return to the project during their next manic phase. Samuel Johnson did his writing during his manic phase. W. Axl Rose, the rock musician, produces frenzied violent music during his manic highs and gentle ballads during his lows.

One study of writers in the USA showed that 80% had mood disorders. A UK study shows that dysfunctionality is more common among all highly creative people than among those who are not creative. Creative people are more sensitive. Sensitive people are more self-analytical and are thus more likely to become unhappy with their lot. This in turn is likely to aggravate any potential for mood disorder which exists. Most psychotic episodes have trigger events such as failing an exam or being criticized by a loved one.

Other functional disorders like autism, do not naturally lend themselves to divergent thinking. Autistic people are constantly looking inward, absorbed in self-centered subjective thought. They are prone to daydreaming, fantasies, hallucinations and delusions, and may find it difficult to apply themselves to exterior problems unconnected with their own well-being. However, not all autistic people are of subnormal psychometric intelligence, although even highly intelligent autists can appear to be, because of their withdrawal from the surrounding world. What most autistic people lack is the ability to put their insights to use in the world, but those who do learn to focus their very high powers of concentration can achieve the extraordinary.

Autistic savants often have much lower than normal IQ levels (between 35 and 75) and yet have very high degrees of skill, usually in one specific area — such as memory, numeracy, music, or art. The best known fictional example of this was the character Dustin Hoffman played in the film *The Rain Man* — a character with quite a high degree of functionality who had both an extraordinary memory and could do instant complex mental calculations. Such savants really do exist. Stephen Wiltshire is perhaps the best known of these, with his ability to produce very detailed architectural drawings from memory. Unlike artists with normal or high creative and psychometric IQ, he is able to do this even months after looking at a building.

Contrary to popular belief, we all indulge in some degree of autistic thinking and in some cases this is when we produce our best ideas. Just before falling asleep or immediately upon waking, for example, it is common for half-remembered dream images and fantasies to merge with waking thoughts, producing highly creative results. This is when eureka experiences occur, and it is often useful to keep a notepad beside the bed to jot down ideas when they occur, before they are swept away in the river of lost dreams.

Male-female differences

On average, men have brains which are slightly larger than the brains of women, but the difference is probably because men, on the whole, are bigger than women. There is no overall IQ differential between men and women. Men are better at spatial and related problems; women are better at verbal-linguistic problems. Interestingly there is a large hormonal component to the differential. During menstruation, when women have low estrogen levels, their spatial cognitive powers can double. They are also more likely to be assertive at this time. Men do best at verbal problems when their testosterone levels are lowest, but are less likely to be assertive at this time. Girls who have been subjected to high levels of testosterone in the womb develop unusually high visual-spatial abilities and other masculine traits.

There are other forces at work here too. Although girls tend to apply themselves more to schoolwork, research has shown that girls taught in an all-girl class do better in related subjects such as science, technical drawing, and maths, than they would if taught in a mixed class. When there are boys present the boys tend to be more pushy than girls and thus attract more of the teacher's time. Thus, although girls are working harder and should do better, they are receiving less teaching time and so do worse. Teachers can do a lot to help balance the books in this area by ensuring that they divide their time equally.

Artificial intelligence

Computers are currently doubling in power every eighteen months and we now have computers which can recognize voices and respond to commands. They have "learned" to react to light and darkness, recognize shapes, communicate with us and with each other, and in some cases, self-repair.

Computers can even write poetry, and recently the first novel by a computer has been published, but this does not mean that computers can think. Not yet anyway. The poetry is not very good, and the novel was not very literate.

Probably the area where computers have the greatest `thinking' success is in chess, but even here we are at a very early stage of development. It took a great deal of human input for IBM's Deep Blue computer to recently beat World Chess Champion Gary Kasparov. And in the sense of humor department, not normally Kasparov's greatest strength, he beat the computer hands down.

Long before Kasparov's encounter with Deep Blue, the British computer scientist Alan Turing looked at the question of whether machines can think and proposed a test of computer IQ which has now been dubbed the Turing test. Turing's test was simple — If you can be fooled by the computer into thinking it is a person, (by communicating through a phone or a keyboard) the computer can be said to think. So far, no computer has ever passed the Turing test when faced with the penetrating questions of an inquisitive human. When a sentence structure that the computer is incapable of answering comes along, computers are programmed to respond by incorporating that word structure or meaning into the answer. For example, if you were to ask the computer, "Tell me why it is better to fall in love than to eat a shrimp," the computer may answer, "Why do you ask me such a foolish question about love and shrimps?"

A human respondent, on the other hand, would be more likely to say, "Love is food for the soul, but a shrimp is food only for the body."

How long will it be before a computer can compare with the wit of Voltaire, who, when told that life is hard, asked, "Compared to what?"

Initially a correspondent may be fooled by the computer's answer, but a number of abstract questions or statements are likely to reveal the computer's lack of thinking depth to a respondent with good human IQ. That said, less intelligent respondents are likely to be fooled by the computer, and with greater computer power and more complex algorithms, the time will come when the average desktop computer will be able to pass the Turing test with ease.

Answers Test Introduction

PUZZLE 1:
37

PUZZLE 2:
20 (2 + 3 + 5 + 10)

PUZZLE 3:
False

PUZZLE 4:
Multitudinous

How can you raise your IQ?

Intelligence is one of the most controversial areas of psychology. For many years people have argued about what it is and how it can be measured. Why is it so difficult? Surely we all know what we expect an intelligent person to be like? But do we? Maybe we have just become used to a rather narrow definition of intelligence.

Suppose, for example, that you lived among a tribe of Amazonian Indians. It is likely that they would value most highly practical abilities such as hunting, fishing and constructing shelters, things that would contribute greatly to the survival of the tribe. The mathematical, verbal and logical skills that we prize so highly would seem to them irrelevant or incomprehensible.

There is a theory that an intelligent Amazonian Indian would, with time, be able to master, say, physics, and that an intelligent Westerner could learn to hunt with a blowpipe and arrows. This is open to debate. It is quite possible that certain behaviours and types of thinking are completely alien to people not familiar with them from infancy.

Though the theory of intelligence is interesting, in practical terms the debate has long been over. The view has taken hold in modern post-industrial societies that people who are quick and accurate at processing data and producing conclusions from that data, possess a valuable ability called "intelligence". Since we know that being able to manipulate words, numbers and concepts can be useful in many contexts, and particularly in the workplace, we make great efforts to identify people who possess that ability to a marked extent. It is the search for such individuals that has given us the IQ test for, whatever its faults, it has been shown that it is a quick and cheap to identify individuals who have something we need.

Since intelligence is so valued, it is in our interests to exhibit as much of it as we can. But can you increase the amount of intelligence you were born with? Psychologists believe not. Once your brain is fully developed, they say, you will possess all the intelligence you are ever going to get. For men this happens in their late teens and for women somewhat earlier. This should mean that, as long as your IQ has been measured by a test that has been constructed, standardised and administered properly, it should not vary during your adult life (though, of course, your faculties might decline during old age).

That, however, is not the end of the story for, in the world of intelligence, something rather odd has been happening. It seems that since the 1950s IQ scores have been rising rapidly. So rapidly, in fact, that someone who had an average IQ 30 or 40 years ago, would be seen as of low intelligence today. Are people really getting brighter with each new generation?

In the mid-1980s James Flynn, professor of political science at the University of Otago in Dunedin, New Zealand showed that IQ scores were rising. It became known as the "Flynn effect". In 1987 Flynn compared IQs across 14 countries. He managed to demonstrate a real growth in IQ scores of up to 25 points in a generation. But what did this mean? Did it really mean that people were becoming more intelligent than their parents? If so, why was there no great flowering of the intellect? Why did we not see a modern version of the Renaissance? Perhaps because what was really happening was just that people were getting better at a certain type of problem solving.

If you think in a certain way for long enough you find, not surprisingly, that you get good at it. For example, anyone who has spent enough time wrestling with so-called lateral thinking puzzles will know that there is a certain sameness about them and, eventually, you get to a stage where you can get the answers quite easily. The same is true of the verbal, numerical, logical, and spatial problems. This practice doesn't make any difference to the total amount of brainpower you possess, but it does have the effect of boosting your IQ score so that, to all intents and purposes, you seem to have become more intelligent.

The tests in this book are designed with exactly this purpose in mind. They will not only familiarise you with types of puzzles that are commonly found in IQ tests, but will help you to solve them and, most important of all, to solve them rapidly.

The tests in this book vary in content. Some are very mixed an aim to give you an impression of what a genuine test would be like. Others are heavily biased towards one sort of question that many people find difficult (for example, if after Test 1, you still can't handle Venn diagrams, I'd be very surprised. We have also put in a large number of spatial puzzles because these are notorious for causing candidates trouble. You will be relieved to hear that the tests are actually harder than the IQ tests you may be subjected to in real life. Marshal Suvarov, a distinguished Russian officer, was famous for saying, 'Train hard, fight easy'. It is a motto worth bearing in mind. If you can work on these tests until they become second nature to you, then there is nothing that an exam can throw at you that you need fear.

The hardest part of IQ tests is staying calm and logical. You need the icy mental processes of a Mr Spock in order to succeed. Above all, never get flustered. If you get bogged down you must move on and try to pick up marks elsewhere. Do not, as I have seen people do, burst into tears and rush from the room. It is not possible to get a high score while sobbing in the loo. All the problems will yield eventually to ab it of logic and persistence, it is your job to work where to apply your efforts in order to get maximum return in the shortest possible time.

How to sit an IQ test

Things that will help and things that won't

Advanced preparation

- When you have completed a test in this book and got your score, go back and try at your leisure all the questions you got wrong or couldn't do at all. Try to get the hang of as many types of question as possible. Practice of this sort will pay off handsomely in the future.
- Take careful note of the questions you are good at and the ones that give you most trouble. This is essential knowledge if you are to use your time effectively in a test.
- Don't waste time trying to get hold of actual tests. They are kept secret and are only sold to people with the proper qualifications. It is quite common for eager test candidates to try to get hold of practice papers but, whether they are motivated by an honest desire to improve their performance or fuelled by the urge to cheat, the answer is always the same.

On the day

- Try to get a good night's sleep before the test. You'll think better if you are not tired.
- Get to the exam well in time. There is nothing so distracting as to rush in at the last moment having got lost in an unfamiliar town.
- If you have a chance to chat to the invigilator and the other candidates before the test, take it. It will help to create a calm and relaxed atmosphere. The invigilator is there to be as helpful as possible, short of actually giving you the answers!
- Chew gum. Seriously, do it! Research has shown that chewing gum aids both concentration and memory. It will also help you to feel relaxed.

The test itself

View an IQ test not like an ordinary exam but like a mental smash and grab raid. This is not a forum in which you are asked to display intellectual virtuosity. It is merely a matter of grabbing as many marks as you possibly can in the time available. And time is of the essence.

IQ tests are frequently designed to allow you insufficient time to complete them. This is not pure sadism on the part of the test compilers, it is a device to prevent what is called the "ceiling effect". If too many people were able to complete the test you run the risk of getting a bunch of people who all get maximum marks and who are not differentiated from each other, even though some are actually more intelligent than others. By making it impossible to complete the test that risk is removed and it is possible to distinguish people who score at, say, the 98th percentile from those who score at the 99th. This method of test construction, however, has implications for everyone, not just for the top scorers. What it means is that, in order to get your maximum score, you need to work as fast as possible and waste no time at all. This does not mean that you should rush and panic, that will only lead to silly mistakes.

First, you should have in your mind a very clear idea of your strengths and weaknesses. If you are good at word problems, but hate maths, then go for those first and leave the maths until later. The tests may well be divided into sections and you will be allowed to complete the sections one at a time. Each section will be given a very precise time for completion and it is imperative that you have a reliable wrist watch to time yourself. When you have, say, a mere eight minutes to complete a section it is vital that you know exactly how much time you have left.

Each section of the test should be treated in the same way. Divide it into four phases:

1. The invigilator will give you detailed instructions before you start and you should listen to these carefully. There is always someone who loses marks simply by not listening. You will probably be nervous so it is essential to make an extra effort to take everything in. Read all the questions and instructions on the exam paper very carefully. Again, someone always manages to get it wrong. Make sure it's not you.

2. As soon as you are allowed to begin, grab any easy marks that are available. There are always easy questions and they do not necessarily all come at the beginning. Go right through the section doing anything that looks easy. Bear in mind that different people find different types of problem simple. It is up to you to hunt out the ones that give you maximum marks quickly.

3. Next settle down to some hard work on the more difficult problems. Examine each problem carefully. If one has five answers (for which you will get five marks), it is probably worth tackling before one that has only a single answer. This is the section that will require the greatest use of your judgment. If a question proves tricky do you give up and try another, or plod on and hope that you crack the one you're on? Only you can tell. But keep an eye on that watch at all times. Again it is important to work first on problems that you find congenial and leave those that you do not much enjoy to last. This book will give you ample opportunity to discover which sorts of problems you thrive on and which tend to defeat you.

4. Finally, when you have just a little time left, dash through all the remaining questions and put down your best guess. There are no penalties for a wrong answer and therefore you can lose nothing by doing this. On the other hand, sometimes your intuitive answers will prove to be correct and sometimes you'll just make a lucky guess. In either case you get more vital marks.

Visual reasoning

It's worth making some special remarks about this subject. It goes under various names: spatial reasoning, and non-verbal reasoning are two that are commonly used. It is important for two reasons. First, it is very popular with people who set IQ tests because it does not depend on previous learning and is therefore considered to be useful in extracting what is called "fluid" intelligence.

There is a well-known test (Raven's Matrices) that is commonly used for young children, among others, for precisely the reason that, even though they might not yet be proficient at reading or maths, they can still complete this vision-based test. Many adults, however, find this sort of test extremely difficult. Taking visual images and manipulating them mentally is a skill that most people find hard to master. In fact, if you were to invigilate IQ tests on a regular basis, you'd soon find that it is this type of test that causes the candidates most pain.

There are two conclusions to be drawn from this. First, pay special attention to questions of this sort and see whether you are a member of the minority who find this sort of reasoning comes naturally. If not, then get as good as you can by constant practice but, should you find that you really do not have the knack of doing this sort of puzzle, relegate them to the category that you attempt last in any test.

The role of memory

You will see that we have included a number of memory tests in this book. Memory has an interesting and useful role to play and it is well worth cultivating your memory "muscles". Although there is no direct link between memory and IQ, there is an indirect link in as much as memory will help you to build up a reservoir of experience about how certain questions are to be tackled.

It is interesting to note that young people will usually be more mentally alert than their elders. The oldies, however, have the benefit of experience, which is really just applied memory. If a young person and an old one both confront a particular problem, the youngster's mind will almost certainly leap into gear first. On the other hand, the oldie will have seen something like this before and will be able to reject a number of ways of dealing with the situation without even trying them. With luck, our senior citizen will remember an analogous situation and will be able to extract from that the necessary information to deal with the new problem.

In the field of IQ testing you must use memory to build up a "reference library" of questions and the methods used to tackle them. This book will provide you with the perfect opportunity to commit to memory a large number of puzzle types that you may well encounter in tests.

Test instructions

You cannot use this book to establish your IQ. That can only be done by a properly constructed test administered under controlled conditions. Use the following tests as a learning experience, a course in how to crack IQ puzzles.

First, try to do each test in no more than ONE HOUR. This is not enough time but it will simulate the way in which IQ tests are administered and will help you to learn how to grab as many points as possible in the time allowed. Set an alarm for the end of the hour and use a watch to keep track of how you are using your time. (In a real test the invigilator will give you a regular time check.)

Choose a quiet place and a time of day when you are unlikely to be disturbed. Much of the value of the test will be lost if you have to break off to, for example, answer the phone. If possible, turn off the ringer for an hour.

When you have completed the test, check your answers against those in the book. Award yourself one point for each correct answer. Where a question has several parts, give yourself a mark for each part. As you go through the book you should find that you are getting more used to the questions are becoming better able to work them out quickly.

Test 1

PUZZLE 1: What letter appears once only in each of the first two words but not at all in the last two words?

1.	FRUITAGE INTERMISSION	INTERPLAY OSTEOPOROSIS	*but not in*
2.	RIPCORD WISTFUL	SHIELDING OCTAGONAL	*but not in*
3.	PINNACLE PINCERS	COMPLAISANT MATCHBOX	*but not in*
4.	IMPLICATION STAMINA	MULTIFORD WARDSHIP	*but not in*
5.	YEOMANLY SPADEWORK	VALENCE CARAMELIZE	*but not in*

PUZZLE 2: Remove one letter from the first word and place it into the second word to form two new words. You must not change the order of the letters in the words and you may not use plurals. What letter needs to move?

1.	SALLOW	BAIL
2.	PITCH	SALE
3.	PRIDE	SLOE
4.	SWAMP	CLAP
5.	STILL	FACE

PUZZLE 3: What word has a similar meaning to the first word and rhymes with the second word?

1.	CRACK	—	DRAKE
2.	BOTTOM	—	CASE
3.	RELAX	—	BEST
4.	TRUMPET	—	CUBA
5.	TRUE	—	MEAL

PUZZLE 4: Look at the shape below and answer the following questions on it.

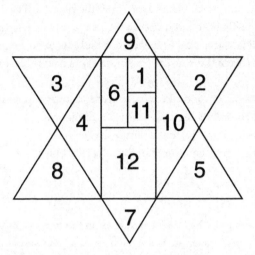

1. How many triangles are there in the diagram?
2. How many rectangles are there in the diagram?
3. How many hexagons can you find?
4. Deduct the sum of the numbers in the rectangles from the sum of the numbers in the triangles.

PUZZLE 5: In the supermarket, the aisles are numbered one to six from the entrance. Washing powder is next to bottles and it is not the first item you see when entering the supermarket. You will see the meat aisle before the bread aisle. Tins are two aisles before bottles and meat is four aisles after fruit.

1. What is in the last aisle (aisle six)?
2. In which aisle can bottles be found?
3. What is in the first aisle?
4. In which aisle can tins be found?

PUZZLE 6: In a car showroom, the white car is at one end of the showroom and the purple car is at the other. The red car is next to the black car and three places away from the blue car. The yellow car is next to the blue car and nearer to the purple car than to the white one. The silver car is next to the red one and the green car is five places away from the blue car. The black car is next to the green car.

1.   Is the silver car or the red car nearer to the purple car?
2.   Which car is three places away from the white car?
3.   Which car is next to the purple car?
4.   Which car is between the silver and the blue?

PUZZLE 7: A survey has been conducted on the types of holidays people have taken over the last twelve months. Five more people had one holiday only and stayed in a self-catering accommodation than had one holiday and stayed in a hotel. Eight people had a camping holiday only and five people took all three types of holiday. Fifty-nine people had not stayed in a hotel in the last twelve months. Four times as many people went camping only as had a hotel and a camping holiday but no self-catering holiday. Of the 107 who took part in the survey a total of 35 people took a camping holiday.

1.   How many people only had a hotel holiday?
2.   How many people stayed in self-catering accommodation and a hotel but did not camp?
3.   How many people did not stay in self-catering accommodation?
4.   How many people stayed in only two of the three types of accommodation?

PUZZLE 8: In a day at the library, 64 people borrowed books. Twice as many people borrowed a thriller only as borrowed a science fiction only. Three people borrowed a biography only and 11 people borrowed both science fiction and a thriller but not a biography. The same number borrowed a biography and a thriller but no science fiction as borrowed one of each of the three types. Twenty-one people did not borrow a thriller. One more person borrowed a science fiction book and a biography book than borrowed a biography only.

1. How many biographies were borrowed in total?
2. How many people borrowed only two of the three types?
3. How many people borrowed a thriller, a biography and a science fiction?
4. How many people borrowed a thriller only?

PUZZLE 9: What word, which is alphabetically between the two given words, answers the clues?

1.	CURIOUS	—	CURRANT	Twist or roll
2.	BARRICADE	—	BARROW	Obstruction
3.	CABRIOLET	—	CAMPAIGN	French town famous for cheese
4.	CALM	—	CALVARY	Unit of energy
5.	DAUGHTER	—	DAY	Beginning

PUZZLE 10: Match the word groups below with the given words.

1. EXTRA
2. WALL
3. VENUS
4. BEND
5. NONE

A	B	C	D	E
Mercury	Zero	Arch	Surplus	Fence
Pluto	Nil	Bow	Excess	Gate
Jupiter	Nought	Curve	Residue	Hedge
Saturn	Nothing	Concave	Remainder	Barrier

PUZZLE 11: Match the word groups below with the given words.

1. WAYNE
2. FOXGLOVE
3. GARNISH
4. TOUGH
5. TWILIGHT

A	B	C	D	E
Dusk	Brando	Durable	Poppy	Trimmings
Sundown	Bogart	Strong	Crocus	Accessories
Sunset	Travolta	Sturdy	Peony	Frills
Nightfall	Swayze	Hardy	Aster	Extras

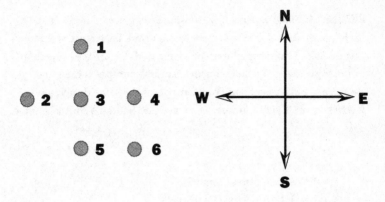

PUZZLE 12: In the map above, C is south of A and south-east of D. B is south-west of F and north-west of E.

1.   Which town is at point 1?
2.   Which town is furthest west?
3.   Which town is south-west of A?
4.   Which town is north of D?
5.   Which town is at point 6?

PUZZLE 13: A certain month has five Wednesdays and the third Saturday is the 18th.

1.   How many Mondays are in the month?
2.   What is the date of the last Sunday of the month?
3.   What is the date of the third Wednesday of the month?
4.   On what day does the 23rd fall?
5.   On what day does the 7th fall?

PUZZLE 14: Three cousins have washing pegged out on the line. On each line there is a shirt, a jumper and a towel. Each has one spotted, one plain and one striped item but none of them has the same item in the same design as their cousins. Sandra's jumper is the same design as Paul's towel and Paul's jumper is the same design as Kerry's towel. Kerry's jumper is striped and Sandra's shirt is spotted.

1. Who has a spotted jumper?
2. What design is Sandra's towel?
3. Who has a striped shirt?
4. What design is Kerry's jumper?
5. What design is Paul's towel?

PUZZLE 15: Three children, Joanna, Richard and Thomas have a pen, a crayon and a pencil-case on their desks. Each has one cat, one elephant and one rabbit design on their item but none has the same item in the same design as the others. Joanna's pencil-case is the same design as Thomas's pen and Richard's pen is the same design as Joanna's crayon. Richard has a cat on his pencil-case and Thomas has an elephant on his pen.

1. Who has a cat on their pen?
2. What design is Richard's crayon?
3. Who has a rabbit on their pencil-case?
4. What design is Thomas's pencil-case?
5. Who has a rabbit on their crayon?

PUZZLE 16: The numbers on the right are formed from the numbers on the left using the same formula in each question. Find the rule and replace the question mark with a number.

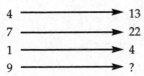

4 ⟶ 13
7 ⟶ 22
1 ⟶ 4
9 ⟶ ?

PUZZLE 17: Can you find a word that begins with the letter "A", which is opposite in meaning to the given word?

1.	VANISH	2.	BELOW
3.	FORFEIT	4.	CONVICT
5.	SWEETNESS		

PUZZLE 18: Can you find a word beginning with the letter "H", which is opposite in meaning to the following?

1.	EXCEPTIONAL	2.	SERIOUS
3.	DIGNIFY	4.	FRIENDLY
5.	DOCILE		

PUZZLE 19

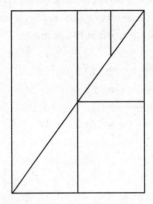

1. How many different sections are there in the drawing?
2. How many triangles are in the drawing?
3. How many rectangles are in the drawing?
4. How many right angles are in the drawing?
5. If the vertical middle line is central, how many similar triangles are there?

PUZZLE 20

	MONKEYS	LLAMAS	LIONS
WILDLIFE PARK A	42	25	16
WILDLIFE PARK B	35	21	14
WILDLIFE PARK C	48	32	10

1. Which park has twice as many monkeys as Park B has llamas?
2. Which park has one quarter of the total lions?
3. At which park does the sum of the llamas and lions total the number of monkeys?
4. Which park has three times as many monkeys as Park A has lions?
5. Which park has twice as many llamas as one of the parks has lions?

PUZZLE 21: In a picture showing a winter scene there are people wearing hats, scarves and gloves. The same number can be seen wearing a hat only as wearing a scarf and gloves only. There are only four people who are not wearing a hat. Five people are wearing a hat and a scarf but no gloves. Twice as many people are wearing a hat only as a scarf only. Eight people are not wearing gloves and seven are not wearing a scarf. One more person can be seen wearing all three than wearing a hat only.

1. How many people are wearing hat, scarf and gloves?
2. How many people are wearing gloves only?
3. How many people are wearing a scarf only?
4. How many people are wearing a hat and gloves but no scarf?
5. How many people are wearing gloves?
6. How many people can be seen in the picture?

PUZZLE 22: In break-time at a shop children can buy chips, candy and soda. Two more children buy candy only than chips only. Thirty-seven children do not buy any candy at all. Two more children buy both chips and soda but no candy than candy only. A total of 60 children buy soda, but only nine of them have soda only. Twelve children buy chips only. One more child buys candy only than candy and soda only, and three more buy both chips and candy but no soda than buy chips and soda but no candy.

1. How many children buy all three items?
2. How many children buy chips and candy but no soda?
3. How many children buy chips and soda but no candy?
4. How many children visit the shop?
5. How many children do not have chips?
6. How many children have candy only?

PUZZLE 23: Sausage, fries and beans are being served to 22 people. The same number have sausage and fries only as sausage and beans only. Only seven do not have fries. The same number have fries and beans only as fries only. Twice as many have beans and sausage but no fries as have sausage only. One person has beans only and one more person has sausage, fries and beans than sausage and fries only.

1. How many people have sausage, fries and beans?
2. How many people have sausage only?
3. How many people do not have beans?
4. How many people do not have sausage?
5. How many people have fries and beans but no sausage?
6. How many people have sausage and fries only?

PUZZLE 24: On sports day the fastest runners are taking part in the sprint, the hurdles and the relay. One more person takes part in the hurdles only than the sprint only. The same number take part in the sprint and the hurdles as take part in the relay and the hurdles. Eleven of the athletes taking some part in these three races do not do the relay. Five people take part in the sprint and the relay and three enter all three races. There are four teams of four runners in the relay. One more person is running in both the relay and the sprint than in the hurdles only.

1. How many people are taking some part in any of the three races?
2. How many people are taking part in the relay only?
3. How many people do not take part in the hurdles?
4. How many people do not take part in the sprint?
5. How many people take part in both the hurdles and relay but not the sprint?
6. How many people take part in two races only?

PUZZLE 25: A survey has been carried out on TV viewing. The survey shows the percentages of people who watch soaps, documentaries and movies. 26% of people watch all three. 39% of people do not watch documentaries. The percentage of people watching soaps only plus the percentage of people watching movies only is the same as the number who watch both movies and documentaries. 27% of people do not watch movies, 14% watch both soaps and documentaries and 3% watch documentaries only.

1. What percentage of people watch both soaps and movies but no documentaries?
2. What percentage watch soaps only?
3. What percentage watch movies and documentaries but not soaps?
4. What percentage watch movies only?
5. What percentage watch only two out of the three types of show?
6. What percentage watch only one type of show?

PUZZLE 26: At a pick-your-own fruit farm, twice as many people are picking raspberries only as plums only. Three more people pick strawberries, raspberries and plums as pick plums only. Four more people pick strawberries only as pick both raspberries and strawberries but not plums. 50 people do not pick strawberries. Eleven people pick both plums and raspberries but not strawberries. A total of 60 people pick plums. If the total number of fruit pickers is 100, can you answer the questions below?

1. How many people pick raspberries?
2. How many people pick all three?
3. How many people pick raspberries only?
4. How many people pick both plums and strawberries but no raspberries?
5. How many people pick strawberries only?
6. How many people pick only two of the three fruits?

PUZZLE 27: At a college teaching crafts, sciences and humanities, the new intake of students can study a maximum of two of the three subjects. One more student is studying a craft and a humanities than a craft only. Two more are studying both a science and a humanities than are studying both a craft and a science. Half as many are studying both a craft and a humanities as are studying both a craft and a science. 21 students are not doing a craft subject. Three students are studying a humanities subject only and six are studying a science only.

1. How many students are not studying a science?
2. How many students are studying both a science and humanities?
3. How many students are studying two subjects?
4. How many students are studying only one subject?
5. How many students are not doing a humanities subject?
6. How many students are studying a craft only?

PUZZLE 28: At a kennel there are Labradors, Alsatians and Greyhounds and also crosses of these breeds. There are two more true Labradors than true Alsatians. Six dogs are Alsatian and Labrador crosses. Ten dogs have no Labrador or Alsatian in them. Only one dog is a mixture of all three breeds. There are twice as many Labrador and Alsatian crosses than Labrador and Greyhound crosses. There is one more Alsatian and Greyhound cross than Labrador and Greyhound cross. Twenty-two dogs do not have any Alsatian in them. There are 40 dogs in total in the kennels.

1. How many true Labradors are there?
2. How many true Alsatians are there?
3. How many true Greyhounds are there?
4. How many Labrador and Greyhound crosses are there?
5. How many Alsatian and Greyhound crosses are there?
6. How many dogs do not have any Labrador in them?

PUZZLE 29: What word has a similar meaning to the first word and rhymes with the second word?

1. FRUIT — GATE 2. PRICE — LOST
3. STOPPER — FORK 4. LEAN — SHIN
5. SPHERE — WALL

PUZZLE 30: The numbers on the right are formed from the numbers on the left using the same formula in each question. Find the rule and replace the question mark with a number.

6 ⟶ 2
13 ⟶ 16
17 ⟶ 24
8 ⟶ ?

Answers | Test 1

PUZZLE 1:

1. A.   **2.** D.   **3.** L.   **4.** 0.   **5.** N.

PUZZLE 2:

1. S, to make Allow, Basil.

2. C, to make Pith, Scale.

3. P, to make Ride, Slope.

4. M, to make Swap, Clamp.

5. T, to make Sill, Facet

PUZZLE 3:

1. Break. **2.** Base. **3.** Rest. **4.** Tuba. **5.** Real

PUZZLE 4:

1.   14.

2.   7.

3.   2 (using segment numbers 1, 6, 7, 9, 11, 12 and 1, 4, 6, 10, 12).

4.   18.

PUZZLE 5:

The aisle order is: 1. fruit, 2. tins, 3. washing powder, 4. bottles, 5. meat, 6. bread.

1. Bread.   **2.** Four.

3. Fruit.   **4.** Two.

PUZZLE 6:

From one end or the other, the order is: white, green, black, red, silver, yellow, blue, purple.

1. Silver.   **2.** Red.

3. Blue.   **4.** Yellow.

PUZZLE 7:

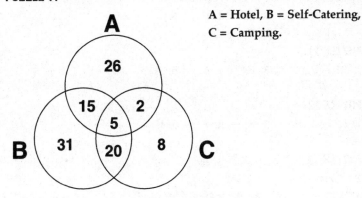

A = Hotel, B = Self-Catering, C = Camping.

1. .26. **2.** 15. **3.** 36. **4.** 37.

PUZZLE 8:

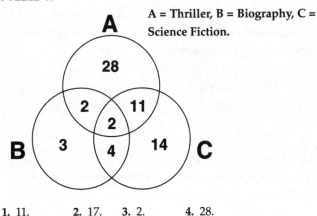

A = Thriller, B = Biography, C = Science Fiction.

1. 11. **2.** 17. **3.** 2. **4.** 28.

PUZZLE 9:

1. Curl. **2.** Barrier.

3. Camembert. **4.** Calorie.

5. Dawn.

Answers Test 1

PUZZLE 10:
1. D.   2. E.   3. A.   4. C.   5. B.

PUZZLE 11:
1. B.   2. D.   3. E.   4. C.   5. A.

PUZZLE 12:
1. F.   2. B.   3. E.   4. F.   5. C.

PUZZLE 13:
1. Four.   2. 26th.
3. 15th.   4. Thursday.
5. Tuesday.

PUZZLE 14:
Kerry has a striped jumper, plain shirt and spotted towel; Paul has a spotted jumper, striped shirt and plain towel; Sandra has a plain jumper, spotted shirt and striped towel.

1. Paul.   2. Striped.
3. Paul.   4. Striped.
5. Plain.

PUZZLE 15:
Joanna has a cat on her pen, a rabbit on her crayon and an elephant on her pencil-case; Richard has a rabbit on his pen, an elephant on his crayon and a cat on his pencil-case; Thomas has an elephant on his pen, a cat on his crayon and a rabbit on his pencil-case.

1. Joanna.   2. Elephant.
3. Thomas.   4. Rabbit.
5. Joanna.

PUZZLE 16:
1. 28. (x 3) + 1

PUZZLE 17:
1. Appear.   2. Above.
3. Acquire.   4. Acquit.
5. Acerbity.

PUZZLE 18:
1. Humdrum.   2. Humorous.
3. Humiliate. 4. Hostile.
5. Headstrong.

PUZZLE 19:
1. 6.   2. 6.   3. 5.   4. 14.   5. 4.

PUZZLE 20:
1. A.   2. C.   3. B.   4. C.   5. C.

PUZZLE 21:

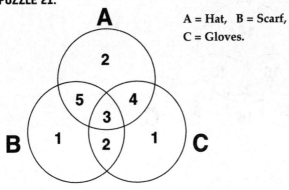

A = Hat, B = Scarf,
C = Gloves.

1. 3.   2. 1.   3. 1.
4. 4.   5. 10.   6. 18.

PUZZLE 22:

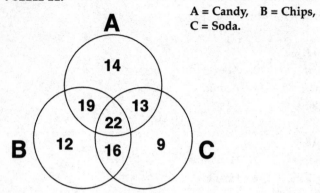

A = Candy,   B = Chips,
C = Soda.

1. 22.   2. 19.   3. 16.
4. 105.   5. 36.   6. 14.

PUZZLE 23:

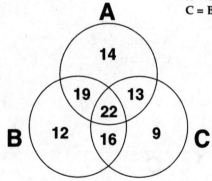

A = Sausage,   B = Fries,
C = Beans.

1. 5.   2. 2.   3. 9.
4. 7.   5. 3.   6. 4.

PUZZLE 24:

A = Sprint,   B = Hurdles,
C = Relay.

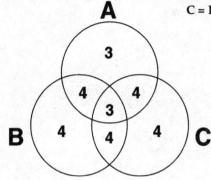

1. 27.   2. 4.   3. 12.
4. 12.   5. 4.   6. 13.

PUZZLE 25:

A = Soaps,   B = Movies,
C = Documentaries.

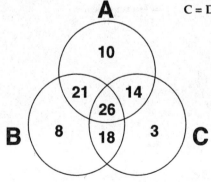

1. 21.   2. 10.   3. 18.
4. 8.   5. 53.   6. 21.

PUZZLE 26:

A = Raspberries,   B = Strawberries,
C = Plums.

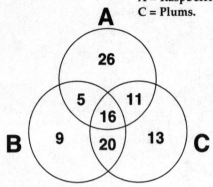

1. 58.   2. 16.   3. 26.
4. 20 .   5. 9.   6. 36.

PUZZLE 27:

A = Craft,   B = Science,
C = Humanities.

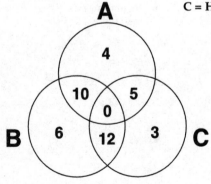

1. 5.   2. 2.   3. 9.
4. 7.   5. 3.   6. 4.

PUZZLE 28:

A = Labrador,   B = Alsation,
C = Greyhound.

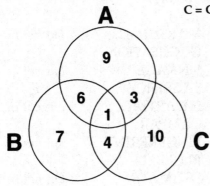

1. 9.   **2.** 7.   **3.** 10.
4. 3.   **5.** 4.   **6.** 21.

PUZZLE 29:

1. Date.   **2.** Cost.
3. Cork.   **3.** Thin.
4. Ball.

PUZZLE 30:

1. 6. (- 5) x 2

PUZZLE 1: What letter appears once only in each of the first two words but not at all in the last two words?

1.	RAMSHACKLE STARDUST	MARSHMALLOW OCCUPATION	*but not in*
2.	PAWNBROKER WONDERFUL	SINKAGE SACRIFICE	*but not in*
3.	WINDSCREEN FICTITIOUS	IMPARTIAL CAMPAIGN	*but not in*
4.	INCRIMINATE ALPINE	FINGERPRINT BLUEBELL	*but not in*
5.	COBBLESTONE GRANITE	ESTIMATE IGNORANCE	*but not in*

PUZZLE 2: Remove one letter from the first word and place it into the second word to form two new words. You must not change the order of the letters in the words and you may not use plurals. What letter needs to move?

1.	WRING	FIST
2.	TWINE	COME
3.	PROUD	BOND
4.	DARTED	BEACH
5.	CURVED	SHOE
6.	CREASE	BAND
7.	BUNGLE	CATER
8.	BRIDGE	FINER
9.	TWAIN	HUNT
10.	STOOP	FLAT

PUZZLE 3: What word, which is alphabetically between the two given words, answers the clues?

1.	DUO	— DUPLICATE	Deceive
2.	EPIC	— EPIGRAM	Widespread disease
3.	EPISODE	— EPITAPH	Letter
4.	FAINT	— FAITH	Fantasy world
5.	FALSE	— FAME	Waver

PUZZLE 4: What word has a similar meaning to the first word and rhymes with the second word?

1.	REAR	—	LACK
2.	HOOP	—	SING
3.	CORROSION	—	MUST
4.	GRIT	—	HAND
5.	THREAD	—	GRAND

PUZZLE 5: Match the word groups below with the given words.

1. JACKET
2. CONSTABLE
3. PUZZLE
4. CHOPIN
5. CUT

A	B	C	D	E
Ernst	Borodin	Reduce	Baffle	Cover
Rembrandt	Vivaldi	Decrease	Bewilder	Wrapper
Dali	Liszt	Lessen	Confuse	Sleeve
Picasso	Elgar	Curtail	Flummox	Envelope

PUZZLE 6: Match the word groups below with the given words.

1. FRANKENSTEIN
2. COUNTRY
3. ANISEED
4. FEELING
5. TRANQUIL

A	B	C	D	E
Calm	Cumin	Kingdom	Werewolf	Theory
Peaceful	Nutmeg	Realm	Demon	View
Restful	Thyme	State	Dracula	Belief
Serene	Saffron	Nation	Vampire	Opinion

PUZZLE 7: The numbers on the right are formed from the numbers on the left using the same formula in each question. Find the rule and replace the question mark with a number.

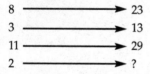

```
8  ----------> 23
3  ----------> 13
11 ----------> 29
2  ----------> ?
```

PUZZLE 8: A farmer keeps only four types of animals. He has a total of 560 animals. If he had 10 sheep less he would have twice as many sheep as he has cows. If he had 10 cows less he would have three cows for every pig, and he has two and one half pigs to every horse.

1. How many pigs does he have?
2. How many horses does he have?
3. If he swaps 75% of his cows for 7 sheep per cow, how many animals will he have in total?
4. How many sheep will he have after the swap?

PUZZLE 9: What numbers should replace the question marks in the series below?

1.   7 9 16 25 41 ?
2.   4 14 34 74 ?
3.   2 3 5 5 9 7 14 ? ?

PUZZLE 10: What number should replace the symbols in this grid if only the numbers 1 to 7 can be used?

□	□	△	○	★	14
★	○	△	○	◉	19
□	○	◉	○	○	23
○	★	◉	★	★	9
○	○	★	■	○	23
16	15	19	18	20	?

PUZZLE 11: What number is missing from this grid?

A	B	C	D	E
7	5	3	4	8
9	8	8	8	8
6	4	9	3	5
8	3	6	?	9

PUZZLE 12: What number should replace the question mark?

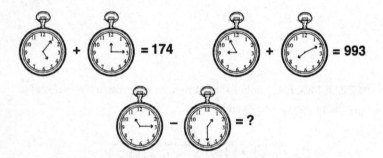

PUZZLE 13: The numbers on the right are formed from the numbers on the left using the same formula in each question. Find the rule and replace the question mark with a number.

6 ⟶ 10
5 ⟶ 8
17 ⟶ 32
12 ⟶ ?

PUZZLE 14: What number is missing from this grid?

A	B	C	D	E
7	8	7	9	7
5	5	8	5	9
6	3	7	3	9
4	4	8	6	?

PUZZLE 15: The numbers in box 1 move clockwise to the positions shown in box 2. In which positions should the missing numbers appear?

1

2	6	7
11		1
10	3	5

2

	10	
7		2
	11	

PUZZLE 16: What number should replace the question mark?

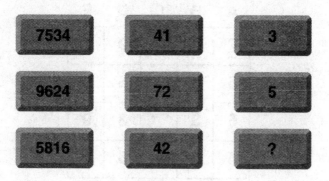

PUZZLE 17: The numbers in box 1 move clockwise to the positions shown in box 2. In which positions should the missing numbers appear?

1

22	15	34
12		14
23	21	19

2

14		12
19		23

PUZZLE 18: What number should replace the question mark?

3569	2307	104
7678	5426	380
9925	4185	?

PUZZLE 19: Complete the analogy.

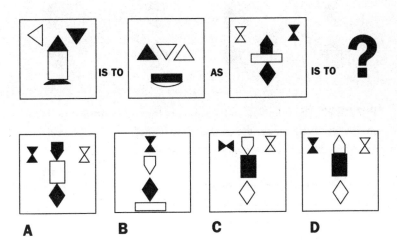

A   B   C   D

PUZZLE 20: The values of grids A and B are given. What is the value of the grid C?

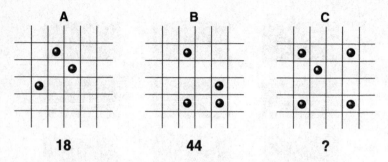

A   B   C

18   44   ?

PUZZLE 21: Can you calculate the number missing in the figure below? Each number is used once only and is not reversed.

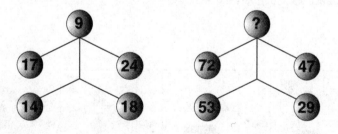

PUZZLE 22: The numbers on the right are formed from the numbers on the left using the same formula in each question. Find the rule and replace the question mark with a number.

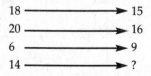

18 ⟶ 15
20 ⟶ 16
6 ⟶ 9
14 ⟶ ?

PUZZLE 23: Starting at the top number, find a route that goes down one level each time until you reach the bottom number.

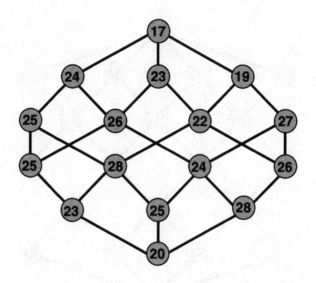

1. Can you find a route where the sum of the numbers is 130?
2. Can you find two separate routes that give a total of 131?
3. What is the highest possible score and what route/s do you follow?
4. What is the lowest possible score and what route/s do you follow?
5. How many ways are there to score 136 and what route/s do you follow?

PUZZLE 24: Starting at the top number, find a route that goes down one level each time until you reach the bottom number.

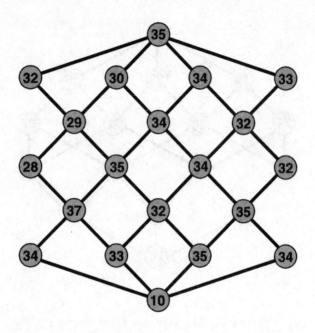

1. Can you find a route where the sum of the numbers is 216?
2. Can you find two separate routes that give a total of 204?
3. What is the highest possible score and what route/s do you follow?
4. What is the lowest possible score and what route/s do you follow?
5. How many ways are there to score 211 and what route/s do you follow?

PUZZLE 25: What is the value of the last string in each of these problems if the first three strings have values as given? Black, white and shaded circles have different values.

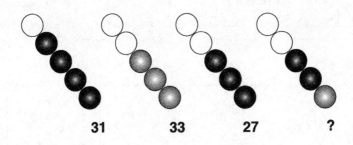

31   33   27   ?

PUZZLE 26: Can you calculate the numbers missing in the figure below? Each number is used once only and is not reversed.

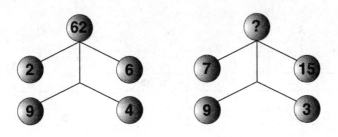

PUZZLE 27: Complete the analogy.

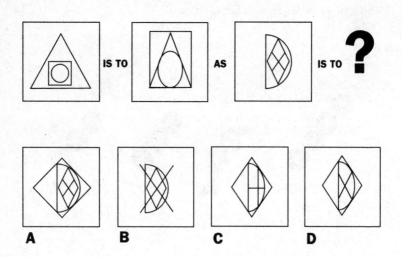

PUZZLE 28: The values of grids A and B are given. What is the value of the grid C?

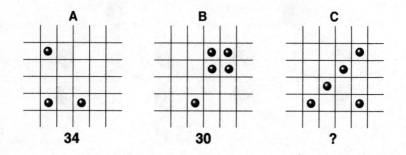

PUZZLE 29: What is the value of the last string if the first three strings have values as given? Black, white and shaded circles have different values.

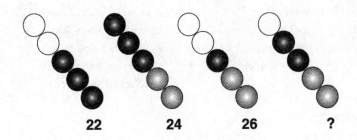

22   24   26   ?

PUZZLE 30: Start at the top-left circle and move clockwise. Calculate the number that replaces the question mark.

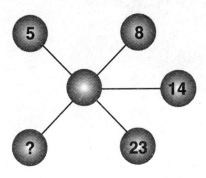

Answers | Test 2

PUZZLE 1:

1. H. **2.** K. **3.** R. **4.** T. **5.** S.

PUZZLE 2:

1. R, to make Wing, First. **2.** T, to make Wine, Comet.
3. U, to make Prod, Bound. **4.** R, to make Dated, Breach.
5. V, to make Cured, Shove **6.** R, to make Cease, Brand.
7. N, to make Bugle, Canter. **8.** G, to make Bride, Finger.
9. A, to make Twin, Haunt. **10.** O, to make Stop, Float.

PUZZLE 3:

1. Dupe. **2.** Epidemic.
3. Epistle. **4.** Fairyland.
5. Falter.

PUZZLE 4:

1. Back. **2.** Ring.
3. Rust. **4.** Sand.
5. Strand.

PUZZLE 5:

1. E. **2.** A. **3.** D. **4.** B. **5.** C.

PUZZLE 6:

1. D. **2.** C. **3.** B. **4.** E. **5.** A.

PUZZLE 7:

11. (x 2) + 7

PUZZLE 8:

1. 50. **2.** 20.
3. 1280. **4.** 1170.

PUZZLE 9:

1. 66. Two previous numbers added.
2. 154. $(n + 3) \times 2$.
3. 9, 20. Two series + 3, + 4, + 5, etc., and + 2 each time.

PUZZLE 10:

□ = 3 △ = 5 ○ = 2 ○ = 7 ● = 4 ★ = 1 ■ = 6

PUZZLE 11:

2. $(A \times B) - (D \times E) = C$

PUZZLE 12:

97. Position of hands (not time) with hour hand, first, expressed as a sum.

$113 - 16 = 97$.

Others are: $51 + 123 = 174$, $911 + 82 = 993$.

PUZZLE 13:

22. $(\times 2) - 2$.

PUZZLE 14:

6. $(BC) + A = DE$

PUZZLE 15:

Move clockwise by the number of letters in the written number.

5		3
1		6

PUZZLE 16:

2. Make sums: First 2 digits – Second 2 digits, then First – Second.

PUZZLE 17:

	21	
15		34
	22	

Move clockwise by the given number minus 1.

PUZZLE 18:

280. First digit x Fourth digit = First and Fourth digits, Second digit x Third digit = Second and Third digits.

PUZZLE 19:

C. White shapes turn 90 degrees clockwise. Black shapes turn 180 degrees. Black and white are reversed.

PUZZLE 20:

40.

4	5	12	13
3	6	11	14
2	7	10	15
1	8	9	16

PUZZLE 21:

37. (Top left + Top right) – (Bottom left + Bottom right).

PUZZLE 22:

13. (÷ 2) + 6.

PUZZLE 23:

1. 17—19—22—24—28—20 = 130   **2.** 17—19—22—28—25—20 = 131
                                        17—23—22—24—25—20 = 131

3. 140. 17—24—26—28—25—20   **4.** 127. 17—19—22—24—25—20

5. 2 ways: 17—24—26—24—25—20
        17—23—22—26—28—20

PUZZLE 24:

1. 35—34—34—34—35—34—10
2. 35—32—29—28—37—33—10
   35—30—29—35—32—33—10
3. 219. 35—34—34—35—37—34—10
4. 202. 35—30—29—28—37—33—10
5. 4 ways: 35—32—29—35—37—33—10
   35—30—34—35—32—35—10
   35—33—32—34—32—35—10
   35—33—32—32—35—34—10

PUZZLE 25:

29. Black = 7; White = 3; Shaded = 9.

PUZZLE 26:

156. (Top left x Bottom right) + (Bottom left x Top right).

PUZZLE 27:

D. Shapes get longer and outside shape moves.

PUZZLE 28:

36.

16	9	8	1
15	10	7	2
14	11	6	3
13	12	5	4

PUZZLE 29:

25. Black = 4; White = 5; Shaded = 6.

PUZZLE 30:

35. (n + 3), (n + 6), (n + 9), etc.

Test 3

Answers on pages 100-103

PUZZLE 1: What letter appears once only in each of the first two words but not at all inthe last two words?

1.	JAVELIN	ABRASIVE	but not in
	PROMPTITUDE	RHOMBUS	
2.	PICTURESQUE	IMMACULATE	but not in
	SITUATION	HIDEOUS	
3.	EDUCATIONAL	MUNDANE	but not in
	STEADILY	RIDGEPOLE	
4.	RICOCHET	GEOLOGICAL	but not in
	OSPREY	POLYCARBON	
5.	ROBUSTIOUS	SPELLBOUND	but not in
	THUNDERCLAP	MOUTHPIECE	

PUZZLE 2: What word, which is alphabetically between the two given words, answers the clues?

1.	DUO	—	DUPLICATE	Deceive
2.	EPIC	—	EPIGRAM	Widespread disease
3.	EPISODE	—	EPITAPH	Letter
4.	FAINT	—	FAITH	Fantasy world
5.	FALSE	—	FAME	Waver

PUZZLE 3: The numbers on the right are formed from the numbers on the left using the same formula in each question. Find the rule and replace the question mark with a number.

$$31 \longrightarrow 12$$
$$15 \longrightarrow 4$$
$$13 \longrightarrow 3$$
$$41 \longrightarrow ?$$

PUZZLE 4: What number is missing from this grid?

A	B	C	D	E
3	5	4	6	3
4	8	5	9	7
6	1	5	4	6
2	2	?	1	4

PUZZLE 5: What numbers should replace the question marks?

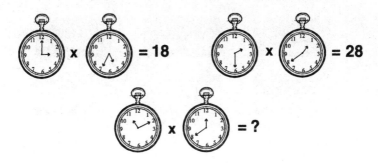

PUZZLE 6: The numbers in box 1 move clockwise to the positions shown in box 2. In which positions should the missing numbers appear?

1

3	5	8
1		6
17	7	9

2

	1	
5		8
	7	

PUZZLE 7: What number should replace the question mark?

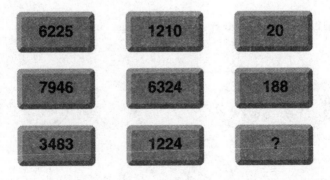

6225	1210	20
7946	6324	188
3483	1224	?

PUZZLE 8: A triangle denotes the grid value and a circle denotes twice the grid value. The values of grids A and B are given. What is the value of the grid C?

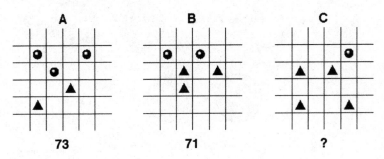

73   71   ?

PUZZLE 9: Can you calculate the numbers missing in the figures below? Each number is used once only and is not reversed.

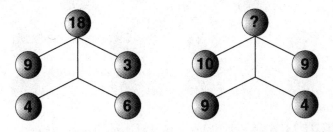

PUZZLE 10: The numbers on the right are formed from the numbers on the left using the same formula in each question. Find the rule and replace the question mark with a number.

31 ⟶ 12
15 ⟶ 4
13 ⟶ 3
41 ⟶ ?

PUZZLE 11: What numbers should replace the question marks?

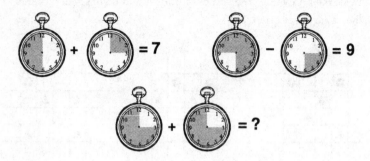

PUZZLE 12: Can you calculate the numbers missing in the figures below? Each number is used once only and is not reversed.

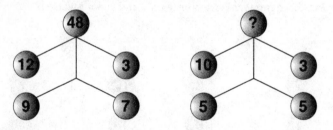

PUZZLE 13: What is the value of the last string in each of these problems if the first three strings have values as given? Black, white and shaded circles have different values.

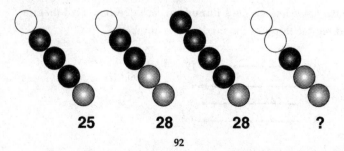

PUZZLE 14: Start at the top-left circle and move clockwise. Calculate the number that replaces the question mark.

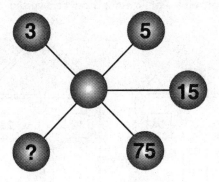

PUZZLE 15: The number in the middle knot of the following bow ties is reached by using all of the outer numbers only once. You cannot reverse the numbers to obtain the answer. Which number should replace the question mark?

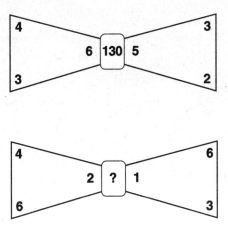

PUZZLE 16: Can you find the missing values on the roofs of the following houses? Each of the numbers on the windows and door must be used only once and no number can be reversed.

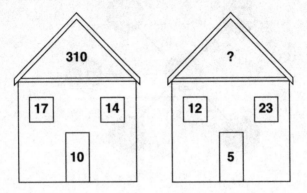

PUZZLE 17: If two-thirds of a number is three-quarters of 422/3, what is that number?

PUZZLE 18: If half the square root of a number is one-fifth of 20, what is that number?

PUZZLE 19: What number is missing from the segments below?

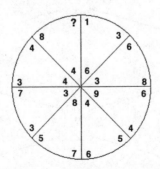

PUZZLE 20: If Alan gives Brenda $5.50 they will both have the same amount of money. If Brenda gives Alan $1.50, Alan will have twice as much as Brenda. What did they have at the start?

PUZZLE 21: A child has an equal number of four different coins from 1c, 5c, 10c, 25c, 50c, and $1. If the total value is $20.28, then how many of which coins does the child have?

PUZZLE 22: You throw three darts at this strange dartboard. How many ways are there to score 50 without a miss and no set of three numbers occurring in a different order?

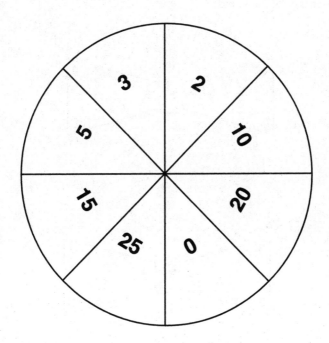

PUZZLE 23: A car is going at 45 mph and is being followed by another car going at 40 mph. If the first car stops after 165m, how long will it take for the second car to catch up?

PUZZLE 24: The number in the middle knot of the following bow ties is reached by using all of the outer numbers only once. You cannot reverse the numbers to obtain the answer. Which number should replace the question mark?

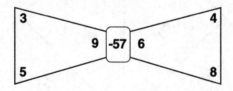

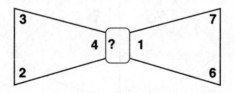

PUZZLE 25: Start at the top-left circle and move clockwise. Calculate the number that replaces the question mark.

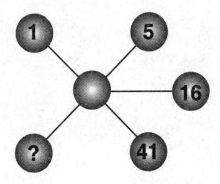

PUZZLE 26: What is the value of the last string in each of these problems if the first three strings have values as given? Black, white and shaded circles have different values.

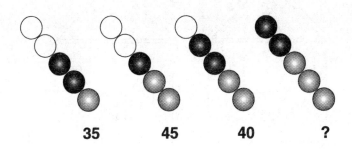

35   45   40   ?

PUZZLE 27: What numbers should replace the question mark?

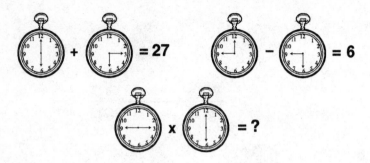

PUZZLE 28: Can you find the missing values on the roof of the right hand house? Each of the numbers on the windows and doors must be used only once and no number can be reversed.

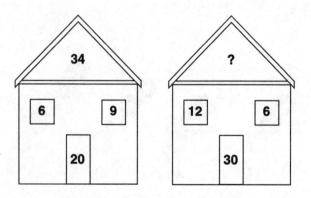

PUZZLE 29: What number is missing from the segments below?

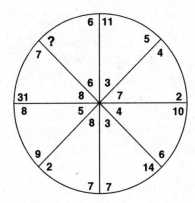

PUZZLE 30: If a quarter of a number is equal to the cube root of 512, what is that number?

Answers | Test 3

PUZZLE 1:

1. V.   **2.** C.   **3.** U.   **4.** I.   **5.** B.

PUZZLE 2:

1. Dupe.   2.   Epidemic.
3. Epistle.   4.   Fairyland.
5. Falter.

PUZZLE 3:

17. $(-7) \div 2$.

PUZZLE 4:

5. (Top row – 3rd row) + 2nd row = 4th row.

PUZZLE 5:

36. Position of hands (not time), expressed as minute hand – hour hand, then do sum. $(2 - 11) [-9] \times (8 - 12) [-4] = 36$.
Others are: $(12 - 3)[9] \times (7 - 5) [2] = 18$, $(6 - 2) [4] \times (8 - 1) [7] = 28$.

PUZZLE 6:

Move clockwise by the given number plus 1.

17	6
9	3

PUZZLE 7:

28. First digit x Second digit = First and Second digits, and Third digit x Fourth digit = Third and Fourth Digits.

PUZZLE 8:

41.

16	9	8	1
15	10	7	2
14	11	6	3
13	12	5	4

PUZZLE 9:

54. (Top left x Bottom left) − (Top right x Bottom right).

PUZZLE 10;

20. (− 7) ÷ 2.

PUZZLE 11:

16. Sum of segment values of shaded parts.

PUZZLE 12:

12. (Bottom left x Bottom right) − (Top left + Top right).

PUZZLE 13.

25. Black = 5; White = 2; Shaded = 8.

PUZZLE 14.

1125. Multiply the previous two numbers.

PUZZLE 15:

120. Sum of left x sum of right.

PUZZLE 16:

175. (Window + Window) x Door.

Answers | Test 3 |

PUZZLE 17:
48.

PUZZLE 18:
64.

PUZZLE 19:
3. Opposite segments total 30.

PUZZLE 20:
Alan $26.50, & Brenda $15.50.

PUZZLE 21:
13 of each 1c, 5c, 50c, 100c.

PUZZLE 22:
5.

PUZZLE 23:
27 minutes & 30 seconds.

PUZZLE 24:
−18. (Left numbers multiplied) − (right numbers multiplied).

PUZZLE 25:
94. $(2n + 3)$, $(2n + 6)$, $(2n + 9)$, etc.

PUZZLE 26:
45. Black = 3; White = 8; Shaded = 13.

PUZZLE 27:

216. Position of hands (not time), added together, then do sum. (3 + 9) [12] x (12 + 6) [18] = 216.

Others are: (12 + 6) [18] + (6 + 3) [9] = 27, (12 + 9) [21] – (9 + 6)[15] = 5.

PUZZLE 28:

42. (Left window x Right window) – Door.

PUZZLE 29:

5. (a x b) – c = d.

PUZZLE 30:

32

Answers on pages 114-117

PUZZLE 1: What word, which is alphabetically between the two given words, answers the clues?

1.	JOG	—	JOKE	Junction of two or more parts
2.	KIOSK	—	KISMET	Smoked fish
3.	LEAF	—	LEAK	An association
4.	LIMBER	—	LIMIT	Rhyme
5.	MEDDLE	—	MEDICAL	Intervene

PUZZLE 2: The numbers on the right are formed from the numbers on the left using the same formula in each question. Find the rule and replace the question mark with a number.

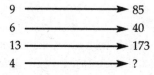

9 ⟶ 85
6 ⟶ 40
13 ⟶ 173
4 ⟶ ?

PUZZLE 3: What word has a similar meaning to the first word and rhymes with the second word?

1.	LINK	—	FOND	2.	INSTRUMENT	—	CARP
3.	FACE	—	TILE	4.	GROOVE	—	BLOT
5.	LOAN	—	SEND				

PUZZLE 4: Can you calculate the number missing in the figure below? Each number is used once only and is not reversed.

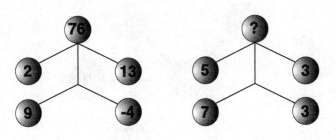

PUZZLE 5: What is the value of the last string if the first three strings have values as given? Black, white and shaded circles have different values.

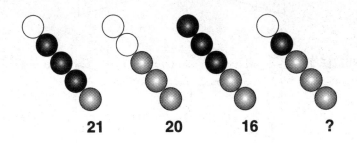

21   20   16   ?

PUZZLE 6: Start at the top-left circle and move clockwise. Calculate the number that replaces the question mark in the following:

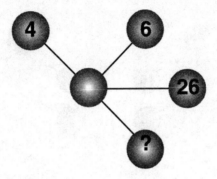

PUZZLE 7: The number in the middle knot of the following bow ties is reached by using all of the outer numbers only once. You cannot reverse the numbers to obtain the answer. Which number should replace the question mark?

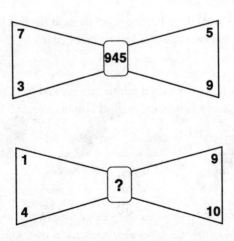

PUZZLE 8: Can you find the missing values on the roof of the right hand house? Each of the numbers on the windows and door must be used only once and no number can be reversed.

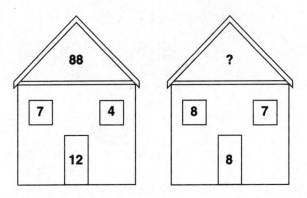

PUZZLE 9: If twice a number is squared and it is equal to one-half of 50, what is that number?

PUZZLE 10: If 3 is subtracted from a number and the remainder is squared, it is 45 less than the original number squared. What was that number?

PUZZLE 11: If 10 times a number is the square root of another number that is 1000 times the number, what is that number?

PUZZLE 12: What number is missing from the segment below?

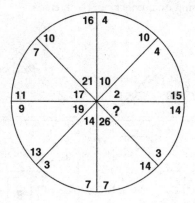

PUZZLE 13: A cube 8in x 8in x 8in is immersed in paint and then cut into half-inch cubes. How many of the cubes will have paint on:

> **(a)** One surface?
> **(b)** Two surfaces?
> **(c)** Three surfaces?

PUZZLE 14: In a small town of 1000 homes, 15% have unlisted telephone numbers and 20% do not have a telephone number at all. If you select 500 numbers from the telephone directory at random, how many of those homes in that town will be unlisted?

PUZZLE 15: Where will the symbols +, −, x and ÷ go if they are used once only to replace the question marks in the following, and what is the highest possible whole number answer?

$$4 ? 2 ? 5 ? 4 ? 9 =$$

PUZZLE 16: Where will the symbols +, −, x and ÷ go if they are used once only to replace the question marks in the following, and what is the highest possible answer?

4 ? 5 ? 6 ? 3 ? 7 =

PUZZLE 17: In each line below match the first given word with the word that is closest in meaning.

	A	B	C	D	E
1. RESCUE	Retrieve	Liberate	Salvage	Redeem	Help
2. PROTESTOR	Rebel	Dissenter	Demonstrator	Marcher	Speaker
3. AGGRAVATE	Anger	Insult	Enrage	Provoke	Instigate
4. ETIQUETTE	Custom	Courtesies	Example	Manners	Protocol
5. INVOLVEMENT	Participation	Concern	Responsibility	Implication	Association

PUZZLE 18: Start at the top-left circle and move clockwise. Calculate the number that replaces the question mark.

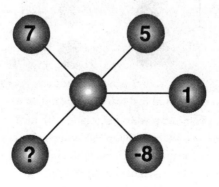

PUZZLE 19: What is the value of the last string if the first three strings have values as given? Black, white and shaded circles have different values.

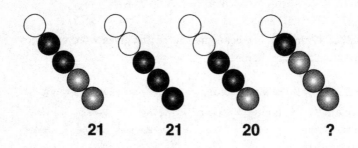

21   21   20   ?

PUZZLE 20: Can you calculate the number missing in the figure below? Each number is used once only and is not reversed.

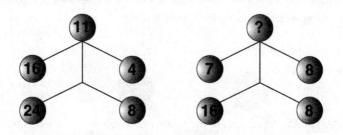

PUZZLE 21: Can you find a word beginning with the letter "H", which is opposite in meaning to the following?

1.   FREE   2.   DESPAIRING
3.   PROSPERITY   4.   VILLAIN
5.   SATISFIED

PUZZLE 22: Can you find a word that begins with the letter "A", which is opposite in meaning to the given word?

1.	PRESENT	2.	IMAGINARY
3.	EXTEND	4.	OPPRESSIVE
5.	IMMATURE		

PUZZLE 23: Make three words that use all of the letters shown.

A   E   G   I   L   N   R   Y

PUZZLE 24: In the following group of words a hidden common connection is present. Can you identify the connection?

1.	NARROWLY	2.	TRAILER
3.	GULLIBLE	4.	JAYWALKING

PUZZLE 25: When each of the following words is rearranged, one group of letters can be used to prefix the others to form longer words. Which word is used as the prefix and what does it become?

	A	B	C	D
1.	RILE	COTS	MUSE	STILE
2.	SHORE	DIE	DUST	TEN
3.	FEATS	LOPE	RYE	BANE

PUZZLE 26: Rearrange the following to form five connected words or names. What are they?

1.   TOUGHDUN   2.   FACETIKUR
3.   BRAGGRINDEE   4.   CAJPALKF
5.   CRANOOMA

PUZZLE 27: Add the vowels in the following groups of letters to form five words, one of which does not belong with the others. Which word is the odd one out?

GLV   HT   SCRF   SHWL   BRCLT

PUZZLE 28: Join the letters of the given words to form a single word using all of the letters.

PEER   +   DAMP

PUZZLE 29: Each of the following words has the prefix missing. The prefix on each question is the same for all of the words in that question. Can you find the prefixes for the following?

_ _ _ DOWY   _ _ _ KING   _ _ _ LLOT   _ _ _ RING

PUZZLE 30: For each word shown write another word with the same meaning beginning with the letter "C".

1.   PSYCHIC   2.   ATROCITY
3.   ACCURATE   4.   OPPOSE
5.   INFORMAL

PUZZLE 31: What number should replace the question mark?

6459	5204	200
7288	5166	360
9768	7422	?

PUZZLE 32: What number is missing from this grid?

A	B	C	D	E
1	5	6	2	7
4	1	5	8	9
7	3	2	6	9
6	2	?	4	?

Answers | Test 4

PUZZLE 1:

1. Joint.   2. Kipper.   3. League.
4. Limerick.   5. Mediate.

PUZZLE 2:

20. (squared) + 4.

PUZZLE 3:

1. Bond.   2. Harp.   3. Dial.
4. Slot.   5. Lend.

PUZZLE 4:

68. (Top left^2 – Bottom right) + (Bottom left^2 – Top right).

PUZZLE 5:

17. Black = 4; White = 7; Shaded = 2.

PUZZLE 6:

666. (n^2 –10) (n = previous number).

PUZZLE 7:

360. All digits multiplied.

PUZZLE 8:

71. (Left window x Door) + Right window.

PUZZLE 9:
2.5.

PUZZLE 10:
9.

PUZZLE 11:
10.

PUZZLE 12:
18. Outside pair added = opposite one inside.

PUZZLE 13:
a) 1176.   b) 168.   c) 8.

PUZZLE 14:
None, only listed numbers will be in the directory!

PUZZLE 15:
27. Divide, plus, minus, multiply.

PUZZLE 16:
26.6. Divide, plus, minus, multiply.

Answers Test 4

PUZZLE 17:
1. C.   2. B.   3. D.   4. D.   5. A.

PUZZLE 18:
–25. (2n – 9) (n = previous number).

PUZZLE 19:
20. Black = 5; White = 3; Shaded = 4.

PUZZLE 20:
9. (Top left x Top right + Bottom left) ÷ Bottom right.

PUZZLE 21:
| 1. | Hold. | 2. | Hopeful. | 3. | Hardship. |
| 4. | Hero. | 5. | Hungry. | | |

PUZZLE 22:
| 1. | Absent. | 2. | Actual. | 3. | Abbreviate. |
| 4. | Airy. | 5. | Adult. | | |

PUZZLE 23:
Relaying, Layering, Yearling.

PUZZLE 24:
Owl, Rail, Gull, Jay

PUZZLE 25:

1. Cost, which makes Costlier, Costumes, Costliest.
2. Stud, which makes Studhorse, Studied, Student.
3. Bean, which makes Beanfeast, Beanpole, Beanery.

PUZZLE 26:

Doughnut, Fruitcake, Gingerbread, Flapjack, Macaroon.

PUZZLE 27:

Bracelet. Others are Glove, Hat, Scarf, Shawl.

PUZZLE 28:

Pampered.

PUZZLE 29:

Sha.

PUZZLE 30:

1.	Clairvoyant.	2.	Cruelty.
3.	Correct.	4.	Counter.
5.	Casual.		

PUZZLE 31:

184. 7 x 2 = 14; 4 x 2 = 8; 184.

PUZZLE 32:

0 and 6. B + D = E; E - A = C.

PUZZLE 1: Can you calculate the number missing in the figure below? Each number is used once only and is not reversed.

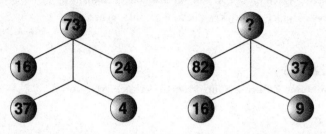

PUZZLE 2: What is the value of the last string if the first three strings have values as given? Black, white and shaded circles have different values.

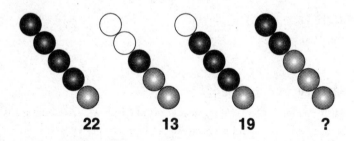

22   **13**   **19**   **?**

PUZZLE 3: Start at the top-left circle and move clockwise. Calculate the number that replaces the question mark.

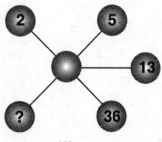

PUZZLE 4: The number in the middle knot of the following bow ties is reached by using all of the outer numbers only once. You cannot reverse the numbers to obtain the answers. Which number should replace the question mark?

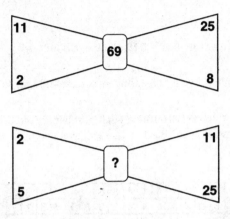

PUZZLE 5: Can you find the missing value on the roof of the right hand house? Each of the numbers on the windows and doors must be used only once and no number can be reversed.

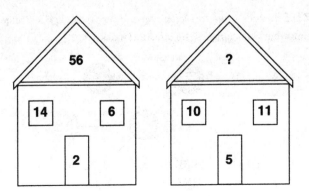

PUZZLE 6: If 26 times a number is 1/26 of 4 x 50, what is that number?

PUZZLE 7: If 40 times a number is half of 7 x 8 x 10, what is that number?

PUZZLE 8: How can 0.18 + 0.19 relate to a lion?

PUZZLE 9: What two whole numbers squared add up to 50?

PUZZLE 10: Can you determine what number should replace the question marks?

2	6	7	9	1				6	1	4	3	8				4	0	3	3	5		
8	0	2	7	6	D	F	A	9	4	4	2	3	B	I	H	?	?	?	?	?	G	C	E
5	3	0	2	4				3	2	6	8	7				1	9	7	8	1		

PUZZLE 11: In each line below match the first given word with the word that is closest in meaning.

	A	B	C	D	E
1. HERMIT	Solitaire	Recluse	Monk	Loner	Hoarder
2. HASSLE	Problem	Nuisance	Worry	Bother	Trouble
3. FICTIONAL	Legendary	Invention	Informal	Genuine	Imaginary
4. EQUIVALENT	Alike	Twin	Equal	Even	Similar
5. FASCINATE	Catch	Charm	Captivate	Occupy	Win

PUZZLE 12: Make three words that use all of the letters shown.

E   N   O   R   S   W

PUZZLE 13: In the following group of words a hidden common connection is present. Can you identify the connection?

MARIGOLDS   JADEDNESS   EPISCOPAL   CHAMBER

PUZZLE 14: When each of the following words is rearranged, one group of letters can be used to prefix the others to form longer words. Which word is used as the prefix and what does it become?

	A	**B**	**C**	**D**
1.	DENT	SON	LYRE	REED
2.	MAD	DEN	SAGE	LESS
3.	TOP	MOOR	EAT	LESS

PUZZLE 15: Rearrange the following to form five connected words or names. What are they?

HETCS   RESSERD   STEETE   BALET   DAWBRORE

PUZZLE 16: Add the vowels in the following groups of letters to form five words, one of which does not belong with the others. Which word is the odd one out?

DNM   KHK   NYLN   SLK   WL

PUZZLE 17: Join the letters of the given words to form a single word using all of the letters.

MEAL   +   DIVE

PUZZLE 18: Each of the following words has the same prefix missing. Can you find the prefix for the following?

    ––– ITAN   _ _ _ PLES   _ _ _ POSE   _ _ _ SUIT

PUZZLE 19: For each word shown write another word with the same meaning beginning with the letter "C".

1. PUNISH   2. SLINGSHOT
3. INEXPENSIVE   4. ANGEL
5. INFANT

PUZZLE 20: Underline the two words that are nearest in meaning?

A	B	C	D	E
Encourage	Indicate	Assure	Suggest	Promise

PUZZLE 21: Which of the following is the odd one out?

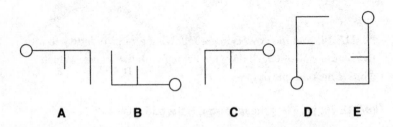

A   B   C   D   E

PUZZLE 22: Which of the following is the odd one out?

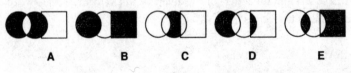

A   B   C   D   E

PUZZLE 23: Which of the following is the odd one out?

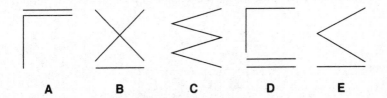

A B C D E

PUZZLE 24: Which of the following is the odd one out?

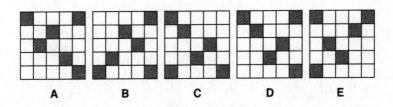

A B C D E

PUZZLE 25: Which of the following is the odd one out?

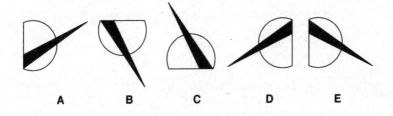

A B C D E

PUZZLE 26: Which of the following is the odd one out?

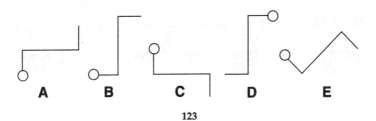

A B C D E

PUZZLE 27: Which of these boxes can be made from the template?
No sign is repeated on more than one side of the box.

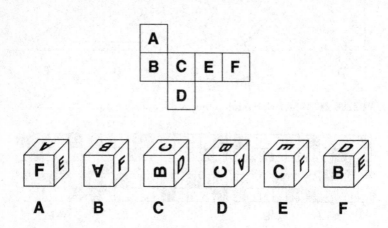

PUZZLE 28: Which of these boxes can be made from the template?
No sign is repeated on more than one side of the box.

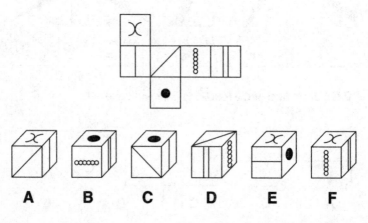

PUZZLE 29: In the puzzle below, which shape should replace the question mark?

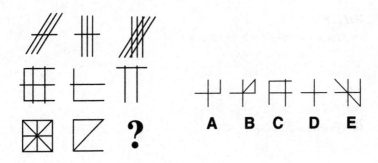

PUZZLE 30: Which of the shapes – A, B, C, D or E – cannot be made from the dots if a line is drawn through all of the dots at least once?

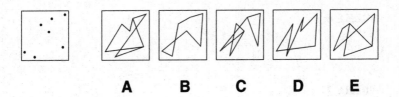

Answers | Test 5

PUZZLE 1:

126. (Top left + Top right + Bottom left) – Bottom right.

PUZZLE 2:

16. Black = 5; White = 2; Shaded = 2.

PUZZLE 3:

104. $(3n – 1)$, $(3n – 2)$, $(3n – 3)$, $(3n – 4)$, etc
(n = previous number).

PUZZLE 4:

360. All digits multiplied.

PUZZLE 5:

60. (Right window – Door) x Left window.

PUZZLE 6:

0.3.

PUZZLE 7:

7.

PUZZLE 8:

Upside down on a calculator 0.37 reads: LEO.

PUZZLE 9:

1 and 7.

PUZZLE 10:

60851. Top row + bottom row + letter values = middle row.

PUZZLE 11:

1. B. **2.** D. **3.** E. **4.** C **5.** C.

PUZZLE 12:

Owners, Worsen, Rowens.

PUZZLE 13:

Gold, Jade, Opal, Amber.

PUZZLE 14:

1. Tend, which makes Tendons, Tenderly, Tendered.

2. Dam, which makes Damned, Damages, Damsels.

3. Tea, which makes Teapot, Tearoom, Teasels.

PUZZLE 15:

Chest, Dresser, Settee, Table, Wardrobe.

PUZZLE 16:

Khaki. Others are Denim, Nylon, Silk, Wool.

PUZZLE 17:

Medieval.

Answers Test 5

PUZZLE 18:
Pur.

PUZZLE 19:
1. Chastise. 2. Catapult.
3. Cheap. 4. Cherub.
5. Child.

PUZZLE 20:
C & E.

PUZZLE 21:
C. Others rotate into the same shape.

PUZZLE 22:
D. A & E and B & C form opposite pairs.

PUZZLE 23:
C. Others are Roman numerals rotated 90° anti- (counter) clockwise.

PUZZLE 24:
D. Others rotate into the same shape.

PUZZLE 25:
E. Others rotate into the same shape.

PUZZLE 26:

A. Others rotate into the same shape.

PUZZLE 27:

C.

PUZZLE 28:

F.

PUZZLE 29:

E. Duplicated lines on first two of each row are deleted in third figure.

PUZZLE 30:

E.

Test 6

Answers on page 140-143

PUZZLE 1: In each line below match the first given word with the word that is closest in meaning.

	A	B	C	D	E
1. THRIVING	Fit	Strong	Wholesome	Flourishing	Nourishing
2. CONFIDE	Entrust	Limit	Secret	Disclose	Speak
3. WANDER	Saunter	Stray	Veer	Drift	Depart
4. NOURISHING	Good	Wholesome	Healthy	Improving	Worthy
5. ESTIMATE	Guess	Roughly	Calculate	Close	Nearly

PUZZLE 2: Rearrange the letters given and make as many words as you can that use all of the letters. At least three words are possible.

B   D   E   N   O   R   S   U

PUZZLE 3: In the following words there is a hidden connection. Can you identify the connection?

DISEASE   BETIDE   UNWAVERING   THREEFOLD

PUZZLE 4: When each of the following words is rearranged, one group of letters can be used to prefix the others to form longer words. Which word is used as the prefix and what does it become?

	A	B	C	D
1.	RED	AND	LEG	RIDE
2.	EMIT	BLEAT	STILE	RILE
3.	SHORE	HOSE	FILES	SHELF

PUZZLE 5: Rearrange the following to form five connected words or names. What are they?

DIALDOFF   PRONDOWS
FUNERSLOW   CHISUFA
GONEIBA

PUZZLE 6: Add the vowels in the following groups of letters to form five words, one of which does not belong with the others. Which word is the odd one out?

PLT   DSH   SCR   CHN   BKR

PUZZLE 7: Join the letters of the given words to form a single word using all of the letters.

HALL   +   SEES

PUZZLE 8: Each of the following words has the same missing prefix. Can you find it?

_ _ _ AWAY   _ _ _ MING   _ _ _ THER   _ _ _ MERS

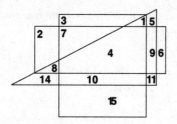

PUZZLE 9: The questions below, 1–5, are about the diagram above.

1. How many numbers 1–15 appear in their own triangle?
2. Of the numbers 1–15, which numbers are missing?
3. Which number/s is/are in all three shapes?
4. From the sum of the numbers appearing in only two shapes, deduct the sum of the numbers appearing in only one shape.
5. If each numbered shape is separated from the whole, how many numbers will not be in a square, rectangle, or triangle?

PUZZLE 10: Underline the two words that are nearest in meaning?

A	B	C	D	E
Assembly	Direction	Presentation	Construction	Preparation

PUZZLE 11: Which of the following is the odd one out?

| A | B | C | D | E |

132

PUZZLE 12: Which of the following is the odd one out?

A   B   C   D   E

PUZZLE 13: Which of the following is the odd one out?

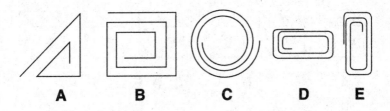

A   B   C   D   E

PUZZLE 14: Which of these boxes can be made from the template? No sign is repeated on more than one side of the box.

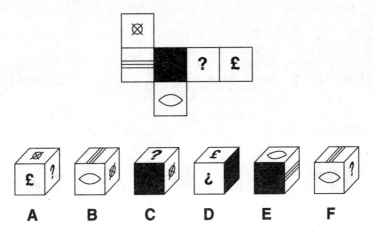

A   B   C   D   E   F

PUZZLE 15: Which of these boxes can be made from the template? No sign is repeated on more than one side of the box.

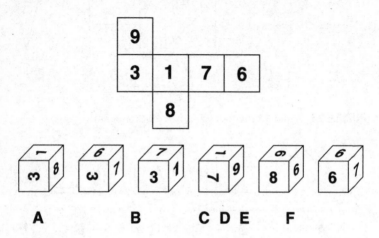

PUZZLE 16: Which of these boxes can be made from the template? No sign is repeated on more than one side of the box.

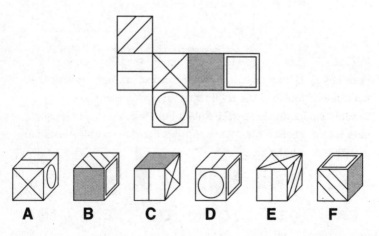

PUZZLE 17: Which of the shapes – A, B, C, D or E – cannot be made from the dots if a line is drawn through all of the dots at least once?

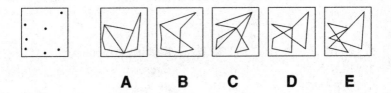

A   **B**   **C**   **D**   **E**

PUZZLE 18: Six people, A, B, C, D, E and F, are in a supermarket queue. F is not at the end of the queue, and he has two people between him and the end of the queue who is not E. A has at least 4 in front of him but is not at the end either. D is not first and has at least two behind him, and C is neither first nor last. List the order of people from the front.

PUZZLE 19: From the information given, find the names and positions of the first eight to finish the marathon. Sean finishes the marathon in fourth place. He finishes after John but before Sandra. Sandra finishes before Robert but after Liam. John finishes after Rick but before Alex. Anne finishes two places after Alex. Liam is sixth to finish the race.

PUZZLE 20: What word, which is alphabetically between the two given words, answers the clues?

   e.g. FLAP (?) FLASH Distress signal from boat (FLARE)

1. LUMP	(?)	LUNCH	Relating to moon
2. MILK	(?)	MIME	Birdseed
3. ESTRANGE	(?)	ETHIC	Endless

PUZZLE 21: Match the word groups below with the given word. Which group completes each line? Answer A, B, C, D or E.

1. YOGHURT
2. TREACHEROUS
3. LIZARD
4. BERNE
5. SCALES

A	B	C	D	E
Anaconda	Butter	Toaster	Dangerous	Cairo
Alligator	Milk	Colander	Threatening	Paris
Terrapin	Cheese	Skillet	Hazardous	Athens

PUZZLE 22: The map below gives the location of 6 towns A, B, C, D, E and F, but they are not in any given order. D is south-west of B and south of E. C is northeast of A and east of F. E is southeast of F and west of B.

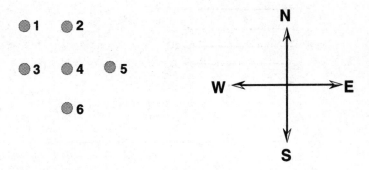

1. Which town is at point 2?
2. Which town is furthest south?
3. Which town is northwest of E?
4. Which town is at point 3?
5. Which town is furthest east?
6. Which town is due south of B

PUZZLE 23: A certain month has five Thursdays in it and the date of the second Sunday is the 13th.

1. What is the date of the third Tuesday?
2. What is the date of the last Friday in the month?
3. What is the date of the first Monday in the month?
4. How many Saturdays are in the month?
5. What is the date of the second Friday in the month?

PUZZLE 24: The numbers on the right are formed from the numbers on the left using the same rules. Discover the rule used and replace the question marks.

3 ⟶ 15
5 ⟶ 23
8 ⟶ 35
9 ⟶ ?

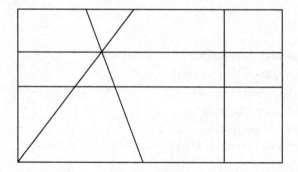

PUZZLE 25: Answer the following questions on the above figure.

1. How many triangles are contained in the drawing?
2. How many right angles can be seen in the drawing?
3. How many sets of parallel lines are there going from side to side or top to bottom?
4. How many different sections are there?
5. How many squares or rectangles are there?

PUZZLE 26: Find a word that begins with the letter R that is opposite in meaning to the given word.

1. FORGETFUL
2. ORDERED
3. OCCASIONAL
4. UNPREPARED
5. CAPTURE

PUZZLE 27: PARIS is to FRANCE as LONDON is to:

JAPAN   AMERICA   GREECE   ENGLAND

PUZZLE 28: NILE is to EGYPT as MAIN is to:

AUSTRIA   FRANCE   ENGLAND   GERMANY

PUZZLE 29: TEN is to PENTAGON as EIGHT is to:

HEXAGON   OCTAGON   SQUARE   TRIANGLE

PUZZLE 30: FLOOD is to RAIN as DULL is to:

SUN   CLOUD   SNOW   ICE

Answers | Test 6

PUZZLE 1:
1. D   2. A.   3. D.   4. B.   5. C.

PUZZLE 2:
Bounders, Rebounds, Suborned.

PUZZLE 3:
Sea, Tide, Wave, Reef.

PUZZLE 4:
1. Dan, which makes Dander, Dangle, Dandier.
2. Time, which makes Timetable, Timelist, Timelier.
3. Horse, which makes Horseshoe, Horseflies, Horseflesh.

PUZZLE 5:
Daffodil, Snowdrop, Sunflower, Fuchsia, Begonia.

PUZZLE 6:
China. Others are Plate, Dish, Saucer, Beaker..

PUZZLE 7:
Seashell.

PUZZLE 8:
Far.

PUZZLE 9:

1. 3.   **2.** 12 and 13.   **3.** 4.
4. −21.   **5.** 4.

PUZZLE 10:

A & D.

PUZZLE 11:

B. A & D and C & E form opposite pairs.

PUZZLE 12:

E. It contains four lines; the others have only three.

PUZZLE 13:

D. The pattern inside does not go clockwise.

PUZZLE 14:

E.

PUZZLE 15:

A.

PUZZLE 16:

F.

Answers Test 6

PUZZLE 17:
A.

PUZZLE 18:
1st, E; 2nd, C; 3rd, F; 4th, D; 5th, A; 6th, B.

PUZZLE 19:
1st, Rick; 2nd, John; 3rd, Alex; 4th, Sean; 5th, Anne; 6th, Liam; 7th, Sandra; 8th, Robert.

PUZZLE 20:
1. Lunar. 2. Millet. 3. Eternal.

PUZZLE 21:
1. B. 2. D. 3. A.
4. E. 5. C.

PUZZLE 22:
1. C. 2. D. 3. F.
4. A. 5. B. 6. None.

PUZZLE 23:
1. 15th. 2. 25th. 3. 7th.
4. Four. 5. 11th.

PUZZLE 24:
39. (x 4) + 3.

PUZZLE 25:
1. 6. **2.** 24. **3.** 9.
4. 12. **5.** 18.

PUZZLE 26:
1. Retentive. **2.** Random. **3.** Regular.
4. Ready. **5.** Release.

PUZZLE 27:
England.

PUZZLE 28:
Germany.

PUZZLE 29:
Square.

PUZZLE 30:
Cloud.

Test 7

Answers on pages 154–157

PUZZLE 1: In each line below match the first given word with the word that is closest in meaning, and record your answer on the answer sheet.

	A.	B.	C.	D.	E.
1. THANKLESS	Unprofitable	Useless	Ungrateful	Worthless	Unsatisfying
2. TRADITIONAL	Fixed	Accustomed	Old	Usual	Age-long
3. APPREHENSION	Distrust	Misgiving	Threat	Wariness	Hunch
4. AMAZE	Bewilder	Confuse	Astonish	Startle	Stagger
5. PROFIT	Earnings	Interest	Revenue	Gain	Value

PUZZLE 2: Make three words that use all of the letters shown.

A   C   D   E   I   L   M   S

PUZZLE 3: These words have a hidden connection. What is it?

CHROME   CORNICE   CLIMATE   BONNIEST

PUZZLE 4: Rearrange the following to form five connected words or names. What are they?

OCAIR   ELOUS   HTAENS   HAGABDD   GANKKOB

PUZZLE 5: Add the vowels in the following groups of letters to form five words, one of which does not belong with the others. Which word is the odd one out?

BNGLW   FLT   HS   GRDN   MSNTT

PUZZLE 6: Join the letters of the given words to form a single word using all of the letters.

RATE   +   RUSE

PUZZLE 7: Each of the following words has the same missing prefix . Can you find it?

_ _ _EVER   _ _ _ DDLE   _ _ _ MACE   _ _ _ PPER

PUZZLE 8: In each question can you underline the two words that are nearest in meaning?

A.	B.	C.	D.	E.
Early	Instant	Alert	Immediate	Efficient

PUZZLE 9: Which of the following is the odd one out?

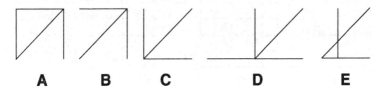

A   B   C   D   E

PUZZLE 10: Which arrangement is missing from these sequences?

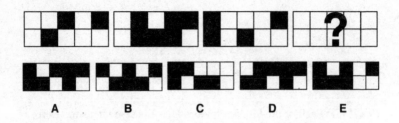

PUZZLE 11: Which arrangement is missing from these sequences?

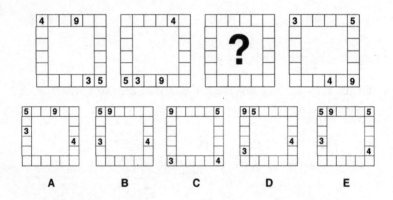

PUZZLE 12: This is a mirror image puzzle. Which of A, B, C or D is the odd one out?

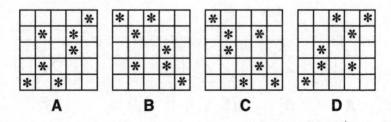

PUZZLE 13: This is a mirror image puzzle. Which of A, B, C or D is the odd one out?

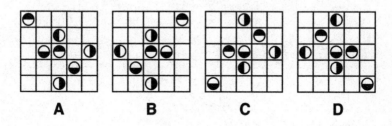

PUZZLE 14: No sign is used on more than one side of the box. Which of these is not a view of the same box?

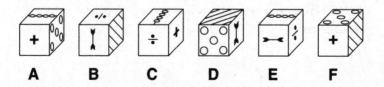

PUZZLE 15: No sign is used on more than one side of the box. Which of these is not a view of the same box?

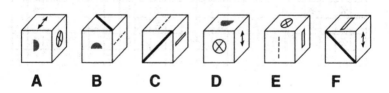

PUZZLE 16: Can you determine which shape has not been used in these questions?

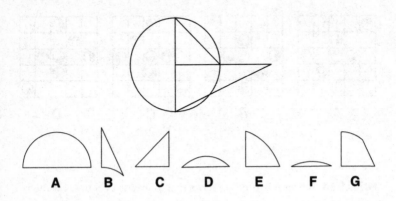

PUZZLE 17: Can you determine which shape has not been used in these questions?

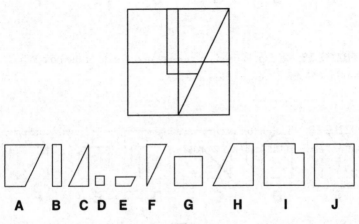

PUZZLE 18: In the puzzle below, which shape should replace the question mark?

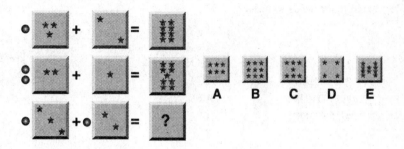

PUZZLE 19: Which of the shapes – A, B, C, D or E – cannot be made from the dots if a line is drawn through all of the dots at least once?

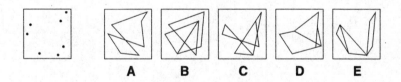

PUZZLE 20: Which letter occurs once in each of the first two words but not at all in the last two words?

RESPECTABLE   PADDOCK   but not in   WATER   PRINT

PUZZLE 21: Remove one letter from the first given word and place it into the second word to form two new words. You must not change the order of the letters in the words and you may not use plurals. What letter needs to move?

1.	WAIST	—	HOOT
2.	PAINT	—	BLOT
3.	TRUST	—	DEER
4.	VITAL	—	ABLE

PUZZLE 22: On each line, place a letter in the brackets that can be attached to the end of the word to the left and to the beginning of the word to the right to form another word in each case. No plurals are allowed.

e.g. COME (T) OWN

1.	LEAN	( )	HIGH
2.	THEM	( )	VERY
3.	SEE	( )	RAFT

PUZZLE 23: What word has a similar meaning to the first word and rhymes with the second one?

1.	BARGAIN	—	MEAL	=
2.	GRAIN	—	HORN	=
3.	PARTY	—	TALL	=

PUZZLE 24: A, B, C, and D take part in school examinations. Only one sits French and that is neither B nor C. B is the only one sitting 3 tests. A sits Math and one other exam. D takes Math and English only. C sits Geography only.

1. Which exam does B not take?
2. Which person sits French?
3. Who takes Math but not English?
4. How many sit two exams?
5. Who sits English but not Geography?

PUZZLE 25: A, B, C, D, and E take part in soccer, baseball, tennis, and swimming, of which soccer is the most popular. More choose tennis than baseball. E only plays one sport. B is the only one to take part in swimming. A and one other of the five play baseball. C does not play soccer. D plays two sports but baseball is not one of them. C plays baseball and tennis.

1. Which sport does A not take part in?
2. Who plays baseball?
3. How many play soccer?
4. Which sport do three of the five take part in?
5. How many play two of the sports only?

PUZZLE 26: What word, which is alphabetically between the two given words, answers the clues?

e.g.   FLAP   (?)   FLASH   Distress signal from boat   (FLARE)

1.	DEPENDENT	(?)	DEPLORE	Exhaust
2.	HERALD	(?)	HERD	Plant-eating animal
3.	CONTEMPT	(?)	CONTEST	Satisfied

PUZZLE 27: Match the word groups below with the given word. Which group completes each line? Answer A, B, C, D or E.

1. REGAL
2. CROWD
3. PYRENEES
4. MISSISSIPPI
5. ORANGE

A	B	C	D	E
Nile	Elegant	Flock	Rockies	Lime
Amazon	Stately	Litter	Alps	Grapefruit
Rhine	Majestic	Gaggle	Pennines	Lemon

PUZZLE 28: Match the word groups below with the given word. Which group completes each line? Answer A, B, C, D or E.

1. TEAM
2. OREGANO
3. BUTTERFLY
4. MUSSEL
5. DALMATIAN

A	B	C	D	E
Lobster	Poodle	Cayenne	Earwig	Pack
Prawn	Whippet	Caraway	Ant	Crew
Crab	Doberman	Garlic	Wasp	Herd

PUZZLE 29: Three neighbors, Harry, Fred, and Paul, each have three cars, one two-door, one four-door, and one five-door. They each own a Buick, a Ford, and a Toyota. None of the same make of cars has the same number of doors. Harry's Buick has the same number of doors as Fred's Ford. Paul's Buick has the same number of doors as Harry's Ford. Harry's Toyota is a two-door and Fred's Toyota is a four-door.

1. Who has a five-door Toyota?
2. Who has a five-door Ford?
3. Who has a two-door Ford?
4. Who has a four-door Buick?
5. Who has a five-door Buick?
6. Who has a two-door Buick?

PUZZLE 30: The numbers on the right are formed from the numbers on the left using the same rules. Discover the rule used and replace the question marks.

3 ⟶ 2
9 ⟶ 6
18 ⟶ 12
24 ⟶ ?

Answers | Test 7

PUZZLE 1:
1. C.   2. B.   3. D.   4. C.   5. D.

PUZZLE 2:
Decimals, Medicals, Declaims.

PUZZLE 3:
Rome, Nice, Lima, Bonn.

PUZZLE 4:
Cairo, Seoul, Athens, Baghdad, Bangkok.

PUZZLE 5:
Garden. Others are Bungalow, Flat, House, Maisonette.

PUZZLE 6:
Treasure.

PUZZLE 7:
Gri.

PUZZLE 8:
B & D.

PUZZLE 9:
E. The others are made of two shapes.

PUZZLE 10:
A. Binary system, start at 5 and add 3 each time. You can also find the answer by treating the images as a negative and mirror-imaging them.

PUZZLE 11:
B. Numbers rotate clockwise by the number given.

PUZZLE 12:
D.

PUZZLE 13:
B.

PUZZLE 14:
D.

PUZZLE 15:
B.

PUZZLE 16:
E.

PUZZLE 17:
G.

PUZZLE 18:
E. • = (numbers of stars x 2) + numbers of stars = number of stars in column 3.

PUZZLE 19:
D.

PUZZLE 20:
C.

PUZZLE 21:
1. S. (Wait – Shoot).
2. A. (Pint – Bloat).
3. T. (Rust – Deter).
4. T. (Vial – Table).

PUZZLE 22:
1. T. Makes Leant and Thigh.
2. E. Makes Theme and Every.
3. D. Makes Seed and Draft.

PUZZLE 23:
1. Deal.
2. Corn.
3. Ball.

PUZZLE 24:
1. French.
2. A.
3. A.
4. Two.
5. D.

PUZZLE 25:
1. Swimming.
2. A and C.
3. Four.
4. Tennis.
5. Three.

PUZZLE 26:

1. Deplete. **2.** Herbivore. **3.** Content.

PUZZLE 27:

1. B.
2. C.
3. D.
4. A.
5. E.

PUZZLE 28:

1. E.
2. C.
3. D.
4. A.
5. B.

PUZZLE 29:

1. Paul.
2. Fred.
3. Paul.
4. Paul.
5. Harry.
6. Fred.

PUZZLE 30:

16. (x 2) ÷ 3.

PUZZLE 1: Make three words that use all of the letters shown.

A   C   E   E   R   R   S   T

PUZZLE 2: In each of the following groups of words a hidden common connection is present. Can you identify the connection?

BARNACLE   CHUTNEY   CRUSHED   CONTENTED

PUZZLE 3: Rearrange the following to form five connected words or names. What are they?

WOIBE   SORS   SCONKAJ   STRANDISE   PLESREY

PUZZLE 4: Add the vowels in the following groups of letters to form five words, one of which does not belong with the others. Which word is the odd one out?

BNGLW   FLT   HS   GRDN   MSNTT

PUZZLE 5: Which arrangement is missing from these sequences?

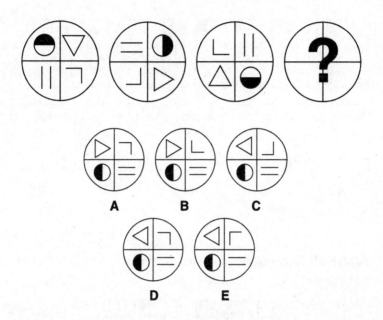

PUZZLE 6: This is a mirror image puzzle. Which of A, B, C or D is the odd one out?

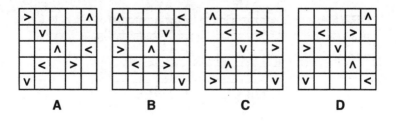

PUZZLE 7: Which arrangement is missing from these sequences?

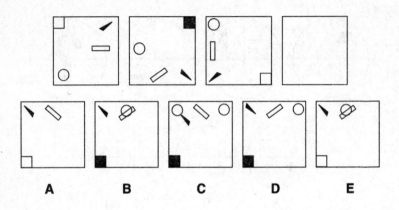

A **B** **C** **D** **E**

PUZZLE 8: This is a mirror image puzzle. Which of A, B, C or D is the odd one out?

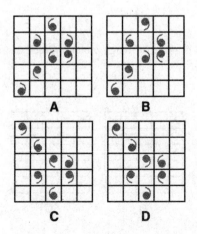

A **B**

C **D**

PUZZLE 9: No sign is used on more than one side of the box. Which of these is not a view of the same box?

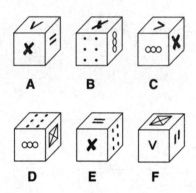

PUZZLE 10: Can you determine which shape has not been used in these questions?

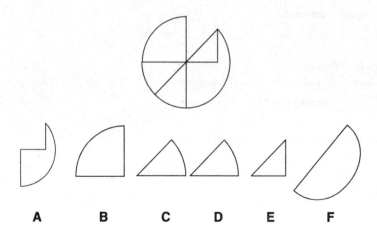

PUZZLE 11: Which of the shapes – A, B, C, D or E – cannot be made from the dots if a line is drawn through all of the dots at least once?

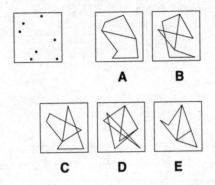

A   **B**

C   **D**   **E**

PUZZLE 12:

What word has a similar meaning to the first word and rhymes with the second one?

1. BRAWL   —   HEIGHT   =
2. RULER   —   SING   =
3. LANTERN   —   RAMP   =

PUZZLE 13: Match the word groups below with the given word. Which group completes each line? Answer A, B, C, D or E.

1. TRIANGLE
2. PHYSICS
3. FILE
4. AEROPLANE
5. COPPER

A	B	C	D	E
History	Saw	Train	Beige	Tripod
Biology	Hammer	Bus	Maroon	Trio
Geometry	Chisel	Car	Violet	Triplet

PUZZLE 14: Maria, Peter and Sarah each have a dog, a cat, and a rabbit, one fluffy-tailed, one short-tailed and one long-tailed. None of the same type of animal has a tail the same as another animal, Sarah's cat has the same type of tail as Peter's rabbit. Maria's rabbit has the same tail type as Peter's cat. Sarah's dog has a long tail, and Maria's cat is fluffy-tailed.

1. Who has a dog with a short tail
2. Who has a rabbit with a long tail?
3. Who has a dog with a fluffy tail?
4. Who has a cat with a short tail?
5. Who has a cat with a long tail?
6. Who has a rabbit with a short tail?

PUZZLE 15: The numbers on the right are formed from the numbers on the left using the same rules. Discover the rule used and replace the question marks.

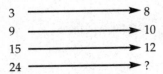

3 ⟶ 8
9 ⟶ 10
15 ⟶ 12
24 ⟶ ?

PUZZLE 16: The table below shows the numbers of medals won by different regions at a sports meeting. Assume every event had a gold, silver, and bronze medal-winner with no tied results.

	GOLD	SILVER	BRONZE
REGION A	33	21	63
REGION B	72	8	20
REGION C	27	60	36

1. Which region won half the number of bronze medals as Region B won in gold medals?
2. Which region won three times as many bronze medals as Region A won in silver medals?
3. Which region won one-fifth of its total in bronze medals?
4. The sum of which two regions' gold medals matched the silver medals won by Region C?
5. If there were two other regions competing and they won only 12 gold medals between them, how many silver medals and bronze medals did they get between them?

PUZZLE 17: HAND is to WRIST as FOOT is to:

KNEE   ARM   CALF   ANKLE

PUZZLE 18: GREEN is to EMERALD as BLUE is to:

DIAMOND   SAPPHIRE   RUBY   GARNET

PUZZLE 19: RABBIT is to BUCK as TURKEY is to:

STAG   COCK   ROOSTER   GANDER

PUZZLE 20: IRIS is to EYE as CILIA is to:

HAIR   SKIN   BONES   TEETH

PUZZLE 21: What number should replace the question mark and what are the values of the symbols?

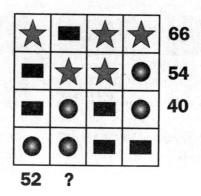

PUZZLE 22: What numbers should replace the question marks in these sequences?

1.	1	5	10	50	100	?	?		
2.	3	8	23	68	?				
3.	3	18	63	198	?				
4.	8	5	4	9	1	7	?	?	?
5.	4	10	22	46	94	?			
6.	6	9	14	21	30	?			

PUZZLE 23: What number should replace the question mark?

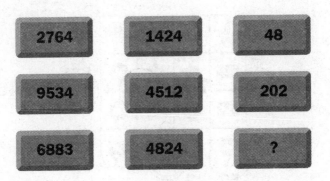

PUZZLE 24: What numbers should replace the question mark in these boxes?

A	B	C	D	E
3	1	4	7	9
7	0	2	8	6
6	5	1	4	7
2	2	3	9	?

PUZZLE 25: What numbers should replace the question marks?

= 735   = 1460

= ?

PUZZLE 26: The values of grids A and B are given. What is the value of the C grid?

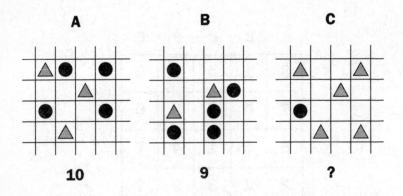

PUZZLE 27: If David gives Mary $4, he will have twice as much as Mary. If Mary gives David $2, David will have 11 times as much as Mary. What did they have at the start?

PUZZLE 28: Using each of the symbols +, −, x and ÷ once only, how can you make the following sum work?   2 ? 6 ? 7 ? 4 ? 9 = 24

PUZZLE 29: If C J is 310 and L P is 1216, what does G R equal?

PUZZLE 30: If D J = 40 and F K = 66, what does H Q equal?

PUZZLE 31: The numbers on the right are formed from the numbers on the left using the same formula in each question. Discover the rule used and replace the question mark with a number.

36	⟶	12
56	⟶	17
12	⟶	6
40	⟶	?

PUZZLE 32: The numbers on the right are formed from the numbers on the left using the same formula in each question. Discover the rule used and replace the question mark with a number.

145	⟶	26
60	⟶	9
225	⟶	42
110	⟶	?

Answers | Test 8

PUZZLE 1:
Retraces, Terraces, Caterers.

PUZZLE 2:
Barn, Hut, Shed, Tent.

PUZZLE 3:
Bowie, Ross, Jackson, Streisand, Presley.

PUZZLE 4:
Garden. Others are: Bungalow, Flat, House, Maisonette.

PUZZLE 5:
E. The figures rotate one sector at a time.

PUZZLE 6:
C.

PUZZLE 7:
B. Shapes rotate in sequence.

PUZZLE 8:
A.

PUZZLE 9:
B.

PUZZLE 10:
F.

PUZZLE 11:
D.

PUZZLE 12:

1.   Fight.
2.   King.
3.   Lamp.

PUZZLE 13:

1.   E.
2.   A.
3.   B.
4.   C.
5.   D.

PUZZLE 14:

1.   Maria.
2.   Maria.
3.   Peter.
4.   Sarah.
5.   Peter.
6.   Peter.

PUZZLE 15:

15. $(\div 3) + 7$.

PUZZLE 16:

1.   C.
2.   A.
3.   B.
4.   A and C
5.   55 silver, 25 bronze.

PUZZLE 17:

Ankle.

PUZZLE 18:
Sapphire.

PUZZLE 19:
Cock.

PUZZLE 20:
Hair.

PUZZLE 21:

42. ⭐ = 17   ● = 5   ■ = 15

PUZZLE 22:
1. 500, 1000. Two methods. Either consecutive Roman numerals or an alternating series, x 5, x 2.
2. 203. Two methods. Either multiply previous number by 3 and deduct 1, or + 5, + 15,   + 45, + 135.
3. 603. (previous + 3) x 3.
4. 6, 3, 2. Numbers 1 to 9 in alphabetic order.
5. 190. (+ 1 (x 2).
6. 41. Two methods. 5 + 12 , 5 + 22, 5 + 32, or series + 3, + 5, + 7, etc.

PUZZLE 23:
328. Along each row multiply first two digits of first number to get first two digits of second number. Multiply last two digits of first number to get last two of second number and join them. 4 x 8 = 32, 2 x 4 = 8; 328.

PUZZLE 24:
3. (A + B) x C = D + E.

PUZZLE 25:
1625. Add times as numbers. 135 + 600 = 735; 245 + 1215 = 1460; 520 + 1105 = 1625.

PUZZLE 26:
Eleven. The values are totalled in each grid to give the number shown. The sum of the values of triangles and circles gives the answer. Δ = 2, O = 1.

PUZZLE 27:
David has $20, Mary has $4.

PUZZLE 28:
(2 + 6) divided by (7 − 4) x 9 = 24.

PUZZLE 29:
718.

PUZZLE 30:
136.

PUZZLE 31:
13. (÷4) ÷3.

PUZZLE 32:
19. (÷5) -3.

Test 9

Answers on pages 188-191

PUZZLE 1: To which group does each of the following words belong?

1. TRAWLER
2. ARTICHOKE
3. CHICKEN
4. TINY
5. HAIL

A	B	C	D	E
Turnip	Snow	Canoe	Minute	Falcon
Pepper	Ice	Dingy	Small	Puffin
Cabbage	Frost	Barge	Short	Pigeon

PUZZLE 2: The numbers on the right are formed from the numbers on the left using the same rules. Discover the rule used and replace the question marks.

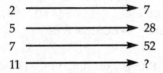

2 ⟶ 7
5 ⟶ 28
7 ⟶ 52
11 ⟶ ?

PUZZLE 3: The numbers on the right are formed from the numbers on the left using the same rules. Discover the rule used and replace the question marks.

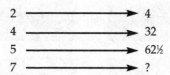

2	⟶	4
4	⟶	32
5	⟶	62½
7	⟶	?

PUZZLE 4: IO is to JUPITER as GANYMEDE is to:

MERCURY　　　SATURN　　　VENUS　　　URANUS

PUZZLE 5: CALORIE is to ENERGY as LUMEN is to:

ELECTRICITY　　PRESSURE　　LIGHT　　HUMIDITY

PUZZLE 6: What number should replace the question mark?

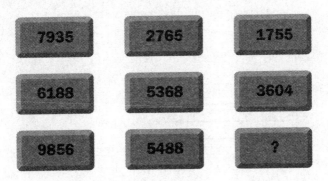

PUZZLE 7: What number should replace the question mark in this box?

A	B	C	D	E
8	2	6	3	4
5	3	4	2	3
9	1	7	3	5
7	6	8	3	?

PUZZLE 8: How many circles are missing from the box with the question mark?

● ●	X	● ●	=	0000
● ●	X	● ●	=	**?**
● ●	+	● ●	=	00
● ●	−	● ●	=	0

PUZZLE 9: What number should replace the question mark?

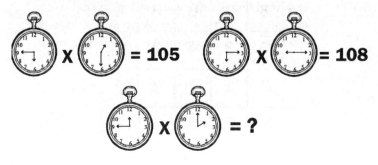

PUZZLE 10: The values of grids A and B are given. What is the value of C grid?

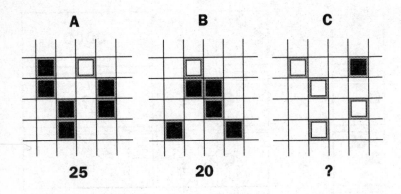

PUZZLE 11: A car has a hole in the base of its fuel tank that leaks petrol at a rate of 1.5 gallons per hour. The car starts with a full tank of fuel (10 gallons) and averages 60 miles per hour until it runs out of fuel. The average fuel consumption, without losses caused by the leak, is 30 miles per gallon. How far will the car travel before it runs out of fuel?

PUZZLE 12: If the hole in the tank on the car above was halfway up the tank, how far would the car have gone?

PUZZLE 13: Which of these boxes can be made from then template?

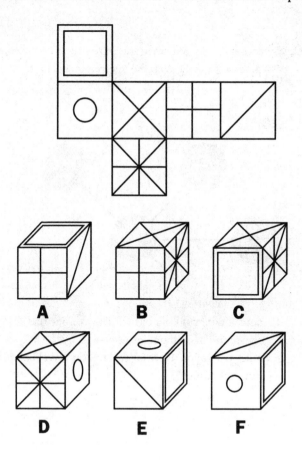

A

B

C

D

E

F

PUZZLE 14: If it is 26 miles to London and 23 miles to Rome, how many miles is it to Moscow?

PUZZLE 15: What three consecutive numbers when squared add up to 365?

PUZZLE 16: Start at the top left circle and move clockwise to find the value of the circle with the question mark in it.

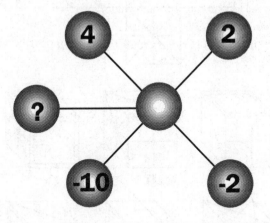

PUZZLE 17: Select a route that takes you from the top number to the bottom number, which always follows a track downwards.

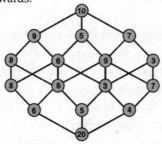

1. Can you find a route which gives you a total of 50?
2. What is the lowest possible route value?
3. What is the second highest route value?
4. How many routes give a value of 43?
5. Can you find a route to give a route value of 49?

PUZZLE 18: What number should replace the question mark?

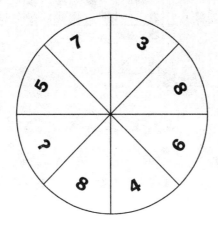

PUZZLE 19: What day of the week has an alphabetical value of 100, if A=1, B=2, and Z=26, when all of the letter values are added together?

PUZZLE 20: My apple tree yielded a good load this year. I swapped half of the apples collected for other fruits and ate 4 apples myself. The next day I swapped half of the remaining apples for some wine and ate a further 3 apples. The next day I ate one apple and gave half of the remaining apples to friends. This left me with 5 apples. How many did I have to start with?

PUZZLE 21: Which of these boxes can be made from the template?

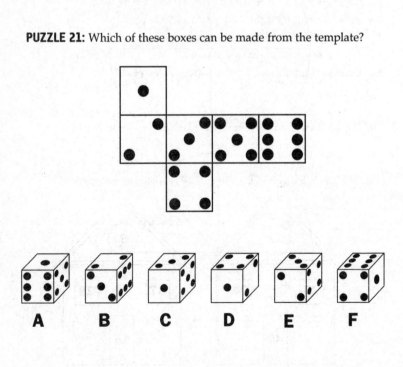

PUZZLE 22: A blacksmith had a surplus of horseshoes. He had bids from between 80 and 100 stables for the 1078 shoes. He wished to divide them equally. How many shoes did each stable get and how many stables were there?

PUZZLE 23: What number should replace the question mark?

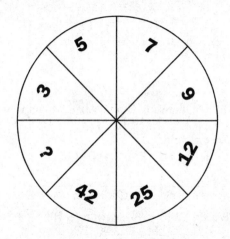

PUZZLE 24: What number should replace the question mark?

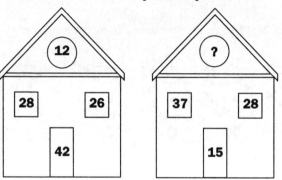

PUZZLE 25: What number should replace the question mark?

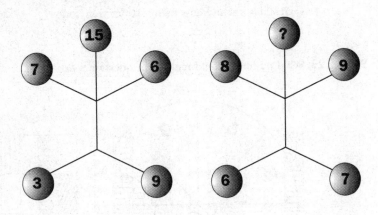

PUZZLE 26: If FACE – DIED = – 67, what does HIDE – BEAD equal?

PUZZLE 27: What number is missing from this sequence:

2.5   4   5   10   25   ?

PUZZLE 28: Complete the analogy.

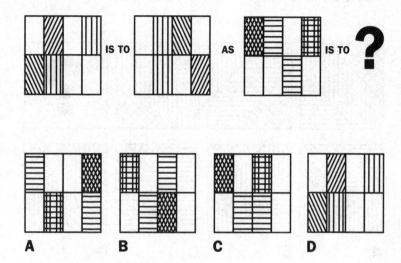

PUZZLE 29: One man can dig a hole in 4 hours. A second man could dig the same hole in 5 hours. A third man could dig the same hole in 6 hours, and a fourth man could dig the same hole in 7 hours. If all of the men worked together to dig the hole, how long would it take to dig to the nearest minute?

PUZZLE 30: Which number completes this sequence:

7   49   441   ?

185

PUZZLE 31: Should A, B, C or D go next in this series?

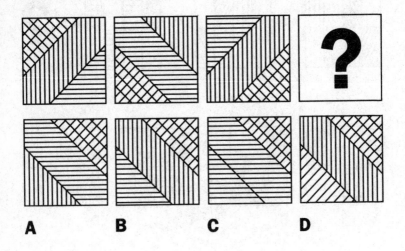

A   B   C   D

PUZZLE 32: What number completes the sum below?

	D	A	M		A	I	L
+	8	8	7	+	?	?	?
	L	I	T		G	O	T

PUZZLE 33: In 20 years' time Mrs Pye will be twice as old as her son. At the present time she is 7 times as old as her son. How old will she be in 15 years' time?

PUZZLE 34: Using all of the outer circled numbers once only, can you find the missing numbers ?

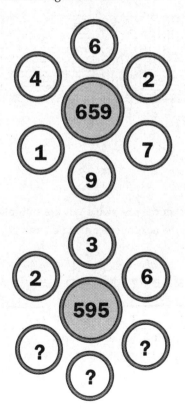

Answers | Test 9

PUZZLE 1:

1. C.

2. A.

3. E.

4. D.

5. B.

PUZZLE 2:

124. $n^2 + 3$.

PUZZLE 3:

1711/2. $n^3 \div 2$.

PUZZLE 4:

Saturn.

PUZZLE 5:

Light.

PUZZLE 6:

4752. In each number the first two digits are multiplied by the last two digits to give the next number along the row. 54 x 88 = 4752.

PUZZLE 7:

3. $(A + C) - (D \times E) = B$ or $A - B + C \div D = E$.

PUZZLE 8:

3 white circles. Black circle values are: Top = 1, right = 2, bottom = 3, left = 4. Values are then added. White circle = 5. Sums are $(1 + 3) \times (4 + 1) = 20$. $(4 + 1) \times (1 + 2) = 15$. $(4 + 1) + (2 + 3) = 10$. $(3 + 4 + 1) - (1 + 2) = 5$.

PUZZLE 9:

294. Add numbers on pointers and complete the sum. (6 + 9) [15] x (1 + 6) [7] = 105; (6 + 3) [9] x (9 + 3) [12] = 108; (12 + 9) [21] x (2 + 12) [14] = 294.

PUZZLE 10:

–15. The sum of the values of white and black squares gives the answer.

 = 5 **= –5**

PUZZLE 11:

171.43 miles.

PUZZLE 12:

235.72 miles.

PUZZLE 13:

A.

PUZZLE 14:

36 miles. Add alphabetical positional values of first and last letters.

PUZZLE 15:

10, 11, 12.

PUZZLE 16:

–26. (n x 2) – 6.

Answers Test 9

PUZZLE 17:

1.	10—5—6—3—5—20.	**2.**	10—7—9—3—5—20.
3.	61: 10—9—8—8—6—20.	**4.**	47: 10—7—3—3—4—20.
5.	3 ways		

10—9—6—6—6—20.

10—7—9—7—4—20.

10—7—9—6—5—20.

PUZZLE 18:

3. Sum of diagonally opposite segments equals 11.

PUZZLE 19:

Wednesday.

PUZZLE 20:

64.

PUZZLE 21:

E.

PUZZLE 22:

11 horseshoes each for 98 stables.

PUZZLE 23:

63. Reading clockwise, the upper half numbers are multiplied by 4, 5, 6, 7, respectively to equal diagonally opposite lower sector.

PUZZLE 24:

50. (Window + window) – door = roof. (37 + 28) [65] – 15 = 50.

PUZZLE 25:

30. (Arm x arm) – (leg x leg) = head. (8 x 9) [72] – (6 x 7) [42] = 30.

PUZZLE 26:

140. The alphanumeric values of each letter are squared and added, then the sum is completed. The sum for FACE – DIED is (62 + 12 + 32 + 52) [71] – (42 + 92 + 52 + 42) [138] = –67; for HIDE – BEAD is (82 + 92 + 42 + 52) [186] – (22 + 52 + 12 + 42) [46] = 140.

PUZZLE 27:

125. Multiply the previous two numbers and divide by 2.

PUZZLE 28:

C. Boxes rotate clockwise and opposite segments are shaded.

PUZZLE 29:

79 minutes. (1 hour 19 minutes).

PUZZLE 30:

441. Multiply last term in each number by the number. (7 x 7), (9 x 49), (441 x 1).

PUZZLE 31:

A. Box rotates 90 degrees anti (counter) clockwise.

PUZZLE 32:

668. Alphanumeric sum. AIL (1, 9, 12) + 6, 6, 8 = 7 (G), 15 (O), 20 (T).

PUZZLE 33:

43 years old. She is currently 28 and her son is 4.

PUZZLE 34:

359. Top number + lower number = middle number. 462 + 197 = 659.

Test 10

PUZZLE 1: Which word is closest in meaning to the given word? Is it A, B, C, D, or E?

	A	B	C	D	E
1. FLAIR	Fashionable	Talent	Style	Able	Quality
2. BONA-FIDE	Correct	Factual	Genuine	Real	Precise
3. ARID	Cold	Desolate	Deserted	Dry	Burnt
4. BOISTEROUS	Carefree	Excessive	Unruly	Evil	Devilish
5. ENDOW	Testament	Probate	Bequeath	Payment	Insurance

PUZZLE 2: Should A, B, C or D come next in the series?

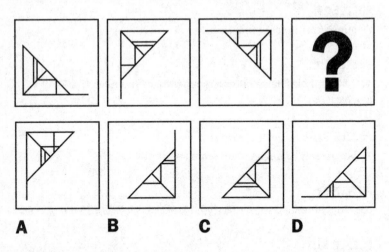

A   **B**   **C**   **D**

PUZZLE 3: Rearrange the following letters to form three words each using all of the letters.

D   E   E   I   R   S   V

PUZZLE 4: In each of the following groups of words there is a hidden common connection. Can you identify the connection?

1.	IMPORTED	COLANDER	FORSAKE	ANTEATER
2.	MINUTES	SELFISHNESS	TRIBUNAL	SHOWPIECE
3.	EXPANSE	RADISH	MUTINY	DEPOT
4.	ENTWINE	MASSAGE	CRUSTATION	KEROSENE
5.	ROMANTIC	GRUFFLY	MOTHER	BEEFBURGER

PUZZLE 5: What, or where am I?

My first is in FIRE but not in GRATE
My second is in EARLY but not in LATE
My third is in MUSIC and also in TUNE
My fourth is in DISTINCT but not in SOON
My last is in FROST and also in SLEET
When ripe, I am juicy and sweet.
What am I?
Where am I?

PUZZLE 6: There have been orders for 200 Rolls Royces, 115 Vauxhalls, and 500 Hondas. How many orders have there been for Renaults?

PUZZLE 7: Should A, B, C or D come next in the series?

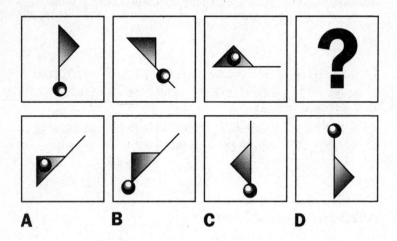

A   B   C   D

PUZZLE 8: Donna has won 500 dance competitions, Patricia has won 102, and Charlotte has won 150. How many competitions has Louise won?

PUZZLE 9: A model shop has ordered 100 kits of cars, 1000 monster kits, and 600 doll kits. How many space-rocket kits did they order?

PUZZLE 10: When each of the following words is rearranged, one group of letters can be used as a prefix for the others to form longer words. Which is the prefix and what does it become?

	A	B	C	D	E
1.	LET	BUS	MILE	RUB	DENT
2.	CHAR	MATS	DIES	NIPS	OPT
3.	SHINES	HIRE	DIE	TIP	SON
4.	EAT	SET	LAP	TAPE	TAME
5.	NIP	LIES	ANT	NOD	NET

PUZZLE 11: Rearrange the following to form five connected words. What are they?

1. ZAMAD	NERTOIC	GUPEETO	TRULEAN	SHIMSTIBUI
2. NIGEAU	KEELSH	TEESAP	COCKEP	ODESUC
3. CUGIC	AGEREJ	DINOM	LENCAH	DIDLELOF
4. TAJECK	HIRST	PRUMEJ	STRUSORE	HOSES
5. MONZAA	GEANGS	SMATHE	TAZEGYN	BAZZEMI

PUZZLE 12: Add the vowels in the following groups of letters to form five words, one of which does not belong with the others. Which word is the odd one out?

	A	B	C	D	E
1.	WLKG	JGGNG	RNNNG	SPRNTNG	STTNG
2.	MSM	MSQ	TMPL	CTHDRL	SYNGG
3.	NSHVLL	SVNNH	LNDN	DTRT	DNVR
4.	MNDY	WDNSDY	JNRY	SNDY	STRDY
5.	RD	YLLW	CRCL	CRMSN	PRPL

PUZZLE 13: Join the letters of the given words to form a single word using all of the letters.

1.	DRUM	+	MIMES		
2.	REPAY	+	LIT	+	SON
3.	DANCE	+	SIT		
4.	SPITE	+	ANTIC		
5.	MEAN	+	ATE		

PUZZLE 14: What, or where am I?

My first is in ACT but not in PLAY
My second is in APRIL but not in MAY
My third is in NOBLE and also in LORD
My fourth is in CARD but not in BOARD
My last is in STACK but not in HAY
You look at me every single day.
What am I?
What am I?

PUZZLE 15: In each of the questions below, 3 pairs of words are given. Match the pair to form 3 longer words.

1. MAIDEN	VENDOR	HAND	MASTER	NEWS	SHIP
2. MAN	PAWN	MASTER	LIVERY	PAY	BROKER
3. SHOOTER	HOUSE	WRITER	SHARP	MASTER	SIGN
4. PLAY	REEL	NEWS	SCREEN	LIGHT	FOOT
5. EVER	DAY	DOMES	WHEN	TAIL	WHITE

PUZZLE 16: For each word shown write another word with the same meaning beginning with the letter G.

1. COLLECT   _ _ _ _ _ _

2. HEREDITARY   _ _ _ _ _ _ _

3. PERMIT   _ _ _ _ _

4. DISTRESS   _ _ _ _ _

5. ELEGANCE   _ _ _ _ _

PUZZLE 17: Which of the following is the odd one out?

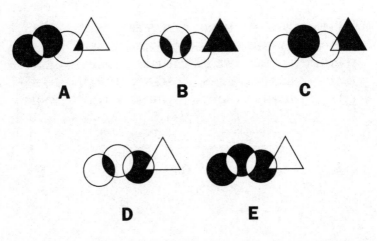

PUZZLE 18: Which of the following is the odd one out?

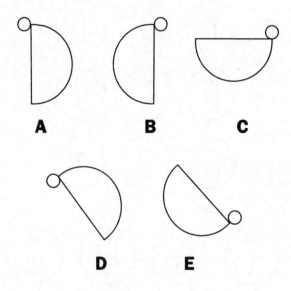

A   **B**   **C**

D   **E**

PUZZLE 19: Which of the following is the odd one out?

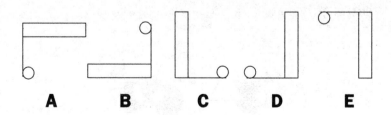

A   **B**   **C**   **D**   **E**

PUZZLE 20: Should A, B, C, or D fill the empty circle?

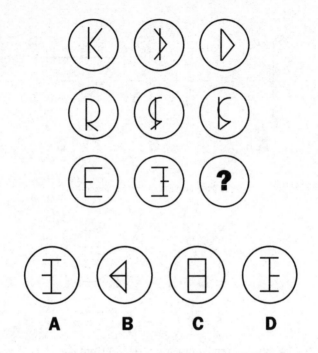

A **B** **C** **D**

PUZZLE 21: Which of the following is the odd one out?

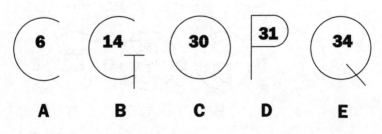

A **B** **C** **D** **E**

PUZZLE 22: No symbol is used on more than one side of the box. Which of these is not a view of the same box?

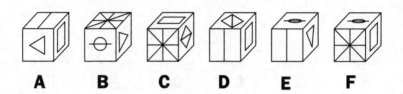

A   B   C   D   E   F

PUZZLE 23: Should A, B, C, or D fill the empty circle?

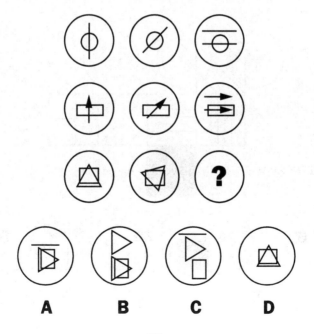

A   B   C   D

PUZZLE 24: No symbol is used on more than one side of the box. Which of these is not a view of the same box?

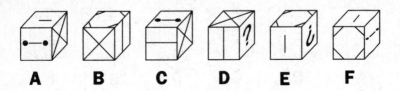

A   **B**   **C**   **D**   **E**   **F**

PUZZLE 25: Which of these boxes can be made from the template? Is it A, B, C, D, E, or F? No sign is repeated on more than one side of the box.

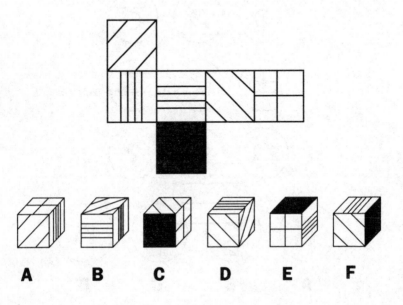

A   **B**   **C**   **D**   **E**   **F**

PUZZLE 26: The numbers on the right are formed from the numbrers on the left using the same simple formula each time. Find the rule and replace the question mark with a number.

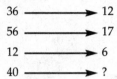

36 ——————➤ 12
56 ——————➤ 17
12 ——————➤ 6
40 ——————➤ ?

PUZZLE 27: The numbers on the right are formed from the numbrers on the left using the same simple formula each time. Find the rule and replace the question mark with a number.

145 ——————➤ 26
60 ——————➤ 9
225 ——————➤ 42
110 ——————➤ ?

PUZZLE 28: The numbers on the right are formed from the numbrers on the left using the same simple formula each time. Find the rule and replace the question mark with a number.

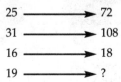

25 ——————➤ 72
31 ——————➤ 108
16 ——————➤ 18
19 ——————➤ ?

PUZZLE 29: What is the value of the last string if the first three strings have values as given? Black, white and shaded circles have different values.

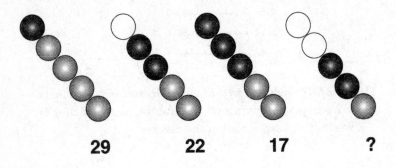

PUZZLE 30: What is the value of the last string if the first three strings have values as given? Black, white and shaded circles have different values.

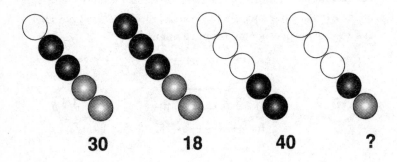

PUZZLE 31: Using all the outer circled numbers once only, can you find the missing number?

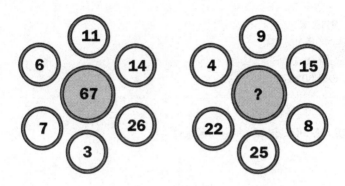

PUZZLE 32: Using all the outer circled numbers once only, can you find the missing number?

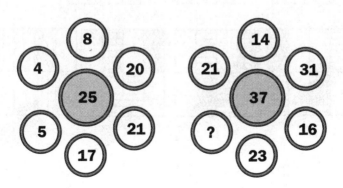

PUZZLE 33: For each word shown write another word with the same meaning beginning with the letter G.

1. WOLVERINE   _ _ _ _ _ _ _
2. STUCK   _ _ _ _ _
3. INORDINATE   _ _ _ _ _
4. LAMENT   _ _ _ _ _ _
5. OPENING   _ _ _

PUZZLE 34: Complete the analogy.

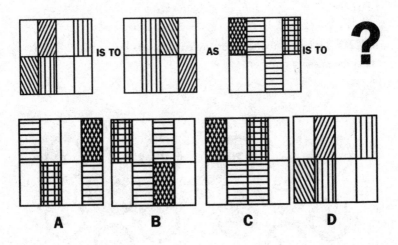

PUZZLE 35: In each of the questions below, 3 pairs of words are given. Match the pair to form 3 longer words.

1.	SPUR	DROP	LILY	LARK	WATER	SNOW
2.	LESS	EARTH	LIST	SACK	QUAKE	RAN
3.	RAM	PEACE	WORD	PART	PASS	ABLE
4.	CRACK	AGE	FOR	BLOCK	WISE	WARD
5.	NAP	HOOD	KID	SOME	FALSE	TROUBLE

PUZZLE 36: Rearrange each group of letters to form three words using all of the letters.

A   D   E   G   N   R

PUZZLE 37: Calculate the values of the black, white, and shaded circles and the sum of the final set in each question.

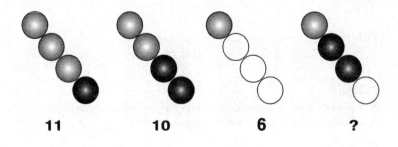

11   10   6   ?

PUZZLE 38: In a studio audience 8 of the guests are from Virginia, 56 are from Pennsylvania, 1 is from Arizona, and 10 are from Texas. How many guests are there from New Mexico?

Answers | Test 10

PUZZLE 1:

1. B. Talent.
2. C. Genuine.
3. D. Dry.
4. C. Unruly.
5. C. Bequeath.

PUZZLE 2:

C. Turns 90 degrees clockwise.

PUZZLE 3:

Derives, Diverse, Revised.

PUZZLE 4:

1. Port, Cola, Sake, Tea.
2. Nut, Fish, Bun, Pie.
3. Pan, Dish, Tin, Pot.
4. Wine, Sage, Rust, Rose.
5. Ant, Fly, Moth, Bee.

PUZZLE 5:

Fruit.

PUZZLE 6:

50. Letters that are Roman numerals in the names are added together.

PUZZLE 7:

B. Turns 45 degrees anti- (counter) clockwise circle moves along.

PUZZLE 8:

51. Letters that are Roman numerals in the names are added together.

PUZZLE 9:

200. Letters that are Roman numerals in the names are added together.

PUZZLE 10:

1. B. SUB. Subtle, Sublime, Suburb, Subtend.
2. E. TOP. Toparch, Topmast, Topside, Topspin.
3. D. PIT. Pithiness, Pithier, Pitied, Pitons.
4. C. PAL. Palate, Palest, Palpate, Palmate.
5. E. TEN. Tenant, Tenpin, Tendon, Tensile.

PUZZLE 11:

1. Mazda, Citroen, Peugeot, Renault, Mitsubishi.
2. Guinea, Shekel, Peseta, Copeck, Escudo.
3. Gucci, Jaeger, Mondi, Chanel, Oldfield.
4. Jacket, Shirt, Jumper, Trousers, Shoes.
5. Amazon, Ganges, Thames, Yangtze, Zambezi.

PUZZLE 12:

1. E. Sitting. The others are Walking, Jogging, Running, Sprinting.
2. A. Museum. The others are Mosque, Temple, Cathedral, Synagogue.
3. C. London. The others are cities in the USA; Nashville, Savannah, Detroit, Denver.
4. C. January. The others are days of the week; Monday, Wednesday, Sunday, Saturday.
5. C. Circle. The others are colors; Red, Yellow, Crimson, Purple.

PUZZLE 13:

1. Midsummer.   2. Personality.
3. Distance.   4. Antiseptic.
5. Emanate.

PUZZLE 14:

Clock.

Answers Test 10

PUZZLE 15:
1. Handmaiden, Newsvendor, Shipmaster.
2. Liveryman, Paymaster, Pawnbroker.
3. Signwriter, Sharpshooter, Housemaster.
4. Screenplay, Newsreel, Footlight.
5. Whenever, Domesday, Whitetail.

PUZZLE 16:
1. Gather.   2. Genetic.
3. Grant.   4. Grief.   5. Grace.

PUZZLE 17:
C. Others are matched opposite pairs.

PUZZLE 18:
B. Others rotate into each other.

PUZZLE 19:
D. Others rotate into each other.

PUZZLE 20:
D. Letter reverses, stick moves to the left.

PUZZLE 21:
D. Number denotes twice the alphabetical position.

PUZZLE 22:
A.

PUZZLE 23:
B. Vertical object moves 45° clockwise, then a further 45° clockwise, then doubles.

PUZZLE 24:
B.

PUZZLE 25:
C.

PUZZLE 26:
13. (÷4) + 3

PUZZLE 27:
19. (÷5) - 3

PUZZLE 28:
36. (-13) x 6

PUZZLE 29:
21. Black = 1, White = 6, Shaded = 7

PUZZLE 30:
47. Black = 0.8, White = 12.8, Shaded = 7.8

PUZZLE 31:
83, Sum of all njumbers in outer circles.

PUZZLE 32:
6. Sum of diagonally opposite numbers is middle number.

PUZZLE 33:

1.	Glutton.	**2.**	Glued.	
3.	Great.	**4.**	Grieve.	**5.**Gap.

PUZZLE 34 :

A. Move sections three places clockwise.

PUZZLE 35:

1. Larkspur, Snowdrop, Waterlily.
2. Listless, Earthquake, Ransack.
3. Rampart, Password, Peaceable.
4. Wisecrack, Blockage, Forward.
5. Kidnap, Falsehood, Troublesome.

PUZZLE 36:

Danger, Gander, Garden, Ranged.

PUZZLE 37:

8. Black = 2; white = 1; shaded = 3.

PUZZLE 38:

1111. Letters that are Roman numerals in the names are added together.

Memory Tests

Memory is of two basic types, short term and long term. The problems you have attempted earlier in the book will have the effect of educating you in certain techniques for problem solving which your mind will automatically store in long term memory. In future, whenever you come across problems similar to these, you will be able to refer to the memories established by your work here and come up with strategies for solving the problems that confront you.

But what of short term memory? Often it is useful to be able to retain complex information for just a short time. For example, if you visit a new town you may want to commit the layout of the streets, including the positions of shops, offices, public buildings and so on, to memory. Unless you propose to visit the town often you will probably not want to remember this information in the long term. You will be quite happy to cram it into your mind for a couple of days and then forget it when you leave.

The following tests will help you develop your short term memory. Remember our earlier discussion about learning styles. If you are a good listener, then read the material over to yourself repeatedly. Make up rhymes or mnemonics that help you to print the facts on your mind. If you are visually adept, then concentrate on drawing pictures and plans that help you to remember. People who like doing things can use tricks such as beating time with a pencil while they commit information to memory.

PROPERTY FOR SALE

The Old Stone House Manor,
Farmhouse Lane,
Hookey,
Worcestershire.

An eye-catching three-storey detached manor house is being sold on the outskirts of Hookey. The property dates back to Elizabethan times and over the last 10 years has been restored considerably, but retains its period atmosphere (including ceiling beams). The property is south-facing with magnificent views over the River Dean and picturesque woodland beyond. There is easy access to the A454 and the B2314.

The property is equipped with gas-fired central heating, double-glazing and a security system.

Offers around **£235,000** are being invited for this freehold home.

The three-storey property has a living room, drawing room, sitting room, breakfast kitchen, utility room, cloakroom and storeroom on the ground floor. On the first floor there are 4 bedrooms (2 with en-suites), and the main bathroom has a spa corner-bath, shower and adjoining dressing room. On the second floor you will find three more bedrooms together with a large games room. There is a large double garage joined on to the property, which is adequate to park three cars.

The property is surrounded by a courtyard, which is well established with a wide variety of shrubs and trees. The borders are well stocked and there is a vegetable patch with potatoes, carrots, lettuces, onions, garlic and broad beans. The property can be viewed by contacting the owners.

1. What is the name of the house?
2. In what town is it situated?
3. Is it in Warwickshire or Worcestershire?
4. How many storeys does the property have?
5. In what part of Hookey will you find the property?
6. In what period was the house built?
7. Does the property have ceiling beams?
8. What is the asking price of the property?
9. Should you contact the agents to view the property?
10. How many bedrooms does the property have?
11. What room adjoins the main bathroom?
12. Does the bathroom have a power shower?
13. How many bedrooms are on the second floor?
14. What two main roads are within easy access to the property?
15. What river can be viewed from the property?
16. Does the property have double-glazing or secondary glazing?
17. Where will you find the games room?
18. What vegetables can be found on the vegetable patch?
19. Is there an orchard?
20. How many cars can you park in the garage?
21. Is the garage joined on to the property?
22. Does the property face south-east?
23. Apart from the river, what else can be viewed from the property?
24. Is there a drawing room on the ground floor?
25. Are there two bedrooms or three bedrooms with en-suites?

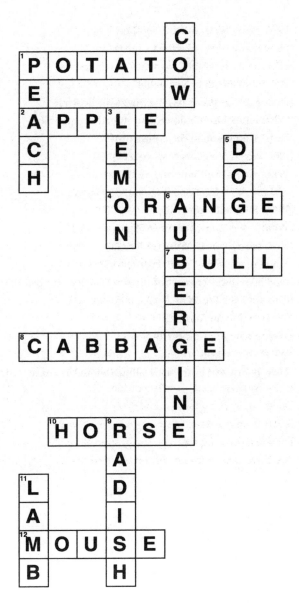

1. How many types of fruit are there?
2. How many types of animals are there?
3. How many types of vegetables are there?
4. Is 3 down a fruit or vegetable?
5. Does cabbage go across the puzzle or down it?
6. What animal is at 5 down and runs through orange?
7. Is there an onion in the crossword?
8. Are there more fruits than vegetables?
9. What animal will you find at 12 across?
10. Is there more than one dog on the crossword?
11. What item will you find at 9 down?
12. What is the longest word in the crossword?
13. How many words have five letters?
14. How many words have three letters?
15. One item in the crossword does not have a number. Which is it?
16. Can apple be found at 2 across or 3 across?
17. Where will you find bull?
18. Where will you find carrot?
19. What animal will you find at 11 down?
20. How many words are there altogether in the crossword?

Study the timetable showing departure time, destination and airline.

DEPARTURE TIME	DESTINATION	AIRLINE
0630	PARIS	BRITISH AIRWAYS
0645	SPAIN	IBERIA
0705	MOMBASSA	MONARCH
0755	FLORIDA	VIRGIN ATLANTIC
0910	CYPRUS	DELTA
0945	IRELAND	AEROFLOT
1000	CHINA	CATHAY PACIFIC
1020	JAMAICA	OLYMPIC
1245	INDIA	KLM
1300	IRELAND	IBERIA
1345	AMSTERDAM	AEROFLOT

1. How many flights are there altogether?
2. At what time is the first flight?
3. What is the destination of the flight that leaves at 09.45?
4. How many flights are there to Ireland?
5. What airline is the flight to Jamaica?
6. Which country are you flying to if you travel by Cathay Pacific?
7. What time does the flight to India leave?
8. Where would you be travelling to if you leave at 07.55 by Virgin Atlantic?
9. What time is the flight to Sydney?
10. What is the name of the airline that leaves at 12.45?
11. If you leave at 12.45, are you going to India or Ireland?
12. How many flights are there to India?
13. How many flights are there by Iberia Airlines?
14. What time is the last flight?
15. Where are you flying if you leave at 10.25?
16. Are there any flights by Aer Lingus?
17. What time is the flight to Spain?
18. If you are travelling to China, do you leave at 10.00 or 10.20?
19. Does the flight to Cyprus leave at 09.10 by Delta Airlines?
20. Does the flight to Jamaica leave at 10.10 by Olympic Airlines?

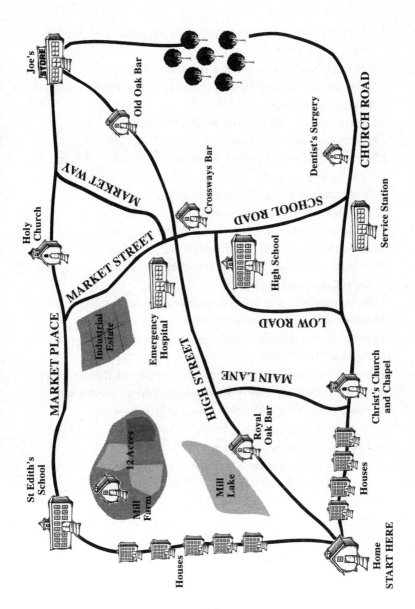

1. What is the name of the road that would take you directly to Joe's store?

2. You decide to start your journey by turning right as you leave your home. Before you reach the church you come to a left turn. What is the name of that road?

3. On what road would you find the Royal Oak bar?

4. How many bars are there on the map?

5. Is there a dentist's surgery on the map?

6. What is the name of the farm on the map?

7. How many acres of land does the farm have?

8. How many churches are there on the map?

9. Can you name the school on Market Place?

10. How many bars are there on High Street?

11. If you travel along High Street from your home, what is the name of the third bar you come to?

12. If you turn left out of your home, how many houses do you pass?

13. Is there a pond or a lake on the map?

14. Which road would you travel down if you needed to fill your car's tank?

15. If you went along High Street, would you take a left or a right to get to the dentist's surgery when you reached the second bar?

16. Name one of the two roads that meet at High School?

17. How many units are on the Industrial Estate?

18. How many roads contain the word "Market"?

19. You turn to the right from your home, pass by Christ's Church and Chapel, and take the next left. What is the name of that road?

20. Which road would you travel along if you wanted to visit Christ's Church and Chapel?

Memory Test 1

1. The Old Stone House Manor.
2. Hookey.
3. Worcestershire.
4. 3.
5. The outskirts.
6. Elizabethan.
7. Yes.
8. £235,000.
9. No.
10. 7.
11. Dressing room.
12. No.
13. 3.
14. A454 and B2314.
15. River Dean.
16. Double-glazing.
17. Second floor.
18. Potatoes, Carrots, Onions, Lettuces, Garlic, Broad Beans.
19. No.
20. 3.
21. Yes.
22. No.
23. Woodland.
24. Yes.
25. 2.

Memory Test 2

1. 4.
2. 6.
3. 4.
4. Fruit.
5. Across.
6. Dog.
7. No.
8. The same.
9. Mouse.
10. No.
11. Radish.
12. Aubergine.
13. 5.
14. 2.
15. Cow.
16. 2 across.
17. 7 across.
18. You will not.
19. Lamb.
20. 14.

Memory Test Answers

Memory Test 3

1. 11.
2. 06.30.
3. Ireland.
4. 2.
5. Olympic.
6. China.
7. 12.45.
8. Florida.
9. There is not one.
10. KLM.
11. India.
12. 1.
13. 2.
14. 13.45.
15. There is not a flight at 10.25.
16. No.
17. 06.45.
18. 10.00.
19. Yes.
20. No.

Memory Test 4

1. High Street.
2. Main Lane.
3. High Street.
4. 3.
5. Yes.
6. Mill Farm.
7. 12 Acres.
8. 2.
9. St. Edith's School.
10. 3.
11. Old Oak.
12. 5.
13. A lake.
14. Church Road.
15. Right.
16. Low Road/School Road.
17. 8.
18. 3.
19. Low Road.
20. Church Road.